FAITHEIST

FaITHeIST

How an Atheist
Found Common Ground
with the Religious

—ɱ—

CHrIS STEDman

Beacon Press, Boston

BEACON PRESS
25 Beacon Street
Boston, Massachusetts 02108-2892
www.beacon.org

Beacon Press books
are published under the auspices of
the Unitarian Universalist Association of Congregations.

15 14 13 12   8 7 6 5 4 3 2 1

This book is printed on acid-free paper that meets the uncoated
paper ANSI/NISO specifications for permanence as revised in 1992.

Text design and composition by Kim Arney

Some names and identifying characteristics of people mentioned
in this work have been changed to protect their identities.

Library of Congress Cataloging-in-Publication Data

Stedman, Chris.
    Faitheist : how an atheist found common ground with the religious /
Chris Stedman.
        p. cm.
    Includes bibliographical references.
    ISBN 978-0-8070-1439-4 (hardcover : alk. paper)
    1. Atheism. 2. Dialogue—Religious aspects. 3. Stedman, Chris.
    4. Spritual biography. I. Title.
    BL2776.S74 2012
    201'.5—dc23   2012022520

For my incredible mom and siblings, and the friends and colleagues who have inspired me to strive for a more loving world by demonstrating compassion and kindness. I'd name you all but that would be a very, very long list.

Also, for the friends who told me that I wouldn't succeed as a rapper—thank you. (But I still might do it someday.)

For small creatures such as we the vastness is bearable only through love.

—CARL SAGAN

Your task is not to seek for love, but merely to seek and find all the barriers within yourself that you have built against it.

—RUMI

Contents

Foreword

There is a moment in the middle of *Faitheist* that nearly took my breath away. Chris is living in Bemidji, a small town in northern Minnesota near the headwaters of the Mississippi River. The nearest big city is Fargo, and it is several hours away. In the winter, the snow piles up so high he can't see out of the bedroom window in his garden apartment.

Chris arrived there hoping to escape his past where, as he writes, "I didn't run into ghosts from my former Christian life that reminded me of the years I spent hating myself for being queer and unable to change it." By the time he was a student at Augsburg College, Chris's disgust with religion had come to define him as deeply as his Evangelical faith once had. To a group of fellow students whom he knew to be believing Christians, he described getting a Bible verse tattooed on his leg as the single stupidest thing he'd ever done, deriving a peculiar pleasure from the offense he caused.

Chris had come to Bemidji because he wanted to live in a place where he could slow down and reflect, form deep relationships with small-town neighbors, and take the first steps down a career path of service. He found a job at a social services agency run by Lutherans (he notes the irony) working as a direct-service professional for adults with developmental disabilities. His closest relationship was with a man named Marvin, who couldn't talk and who could barely sign. He and Chris found other ways to communicate. Marvin would pretend to sock Chris in the jaw, and Chris would fall down and bounce back with his dukes up and say, "This isn't over yet, buddy," sending Marvin into gales of laughter. Chris watched movies with Marvin, sat with him for hours just keeping him company, read to him from his favorite books.

One day, Marvin brought Chris into his room and placed in his hands one of his most precious possessions, his prayer book. He wanted Chris to read from it. Chris hesitated for a second. Perhaps he was reminded of all those nights he lay awake searching the Scripture for verses in the hope of finding one that would make him feel loved for what God made him. Perhaps he was reminded of the time when, in a drunken rage, he kicked in the glass panel of a church sign. But neither longing nor anger overcame him now. This moment was about what it means to be a friend, about expressing care for something Marvin values. Chris read Marvin a prayer. Marvin, normally tense, let his arms relax. Perhaps he sensed that some deep personal bridge had been crossed in his presence. He pressed his face tightly against Chris's blue flannel shirt and kept it there for a long time.

—∿—

One struggles to imagine the late Christopher Hitchens performing that intimate act of mercy. Or Sam Harris or Daniel Dennett or Richard Dawkins or any of the other prominent so-called New Atheists you've likely heard of.

Chris Stedman is different from the atheists who wear that badge on TV (Bill Maher comes to mind). His atheism doesn't hate God; it loves people. He is proud of who he is (gay, atheist, Minnesotan, heavily tattooed, staff member at the Harvard Humanist Association, writer), and he wants to create a world where all people are free to be proud of who they are—Muslim, Jew, Hindu, Sikh, atheist, wanderer, whatever. He believes that the atheist movement ought to be talking more about what it does stand for than what it doesn't. He believes energy spent disparaging what others believe is worse than wasteful; it's toxic. His goal is to nurture a movement of Humanists who emphasize cultivating humanity, express it in serving others, and work with people of all faiths, in good faith, towards that end. Chris understands that we get there together or not at all.

Like all good personal stories, *Faitheist* casts light on an important dimension of our public life. In this case, it is the growing chasm between believers and atheists. It was a chasm first opened by believers, who have mercilessly berated and bullied nonbelievers in ways antithetical to the values of respect, compassion, and freedom central to all our faiths. In recent years, a small, loud group of atheists have battled back, with choice quotes like this one from PZ Myers: "I say, screw the polite words. . . . Break out the steel-toed boots and brass knuckles, and get out there and hammer on the lunatics and idiots."[1]

There's a set of religious people out there who are only too happy to return the same violent language, and probably more likely to employ the actual tactics.

The wider the chasm, the longer the bridge you're going to need to cross it. This book is a piece of that bridge for our broader culture. And what's more, there are tools and skills and stories in these pages that will be useful to bridge builders of all backgrounds.

—∞—

Here is another thing good personal stories do: help readers narrate their own lives alongside the life unfolding in the pages of the book. Reading *Faitheist* brought back memories I had long buried. In one scene, Chris writes about being out on the town with a group of friends when they are verbally accosted by people shouting, "Fags! Repent!" Chris nods to his friends to keep walking while he stands on the street corner and allows the group to preach at him. He listens politely, joining in when he hears a Bible verse he recognizes, and then asks if he can share his story. The men are a little shocked but as Chris has listened with such grace, they seem to think it's only fair to let him have his say. And so Chris speaks of his years as a Christian, his coming out, his undergraduate degree in religion, his becoming an atheist, his current graduate study at a seminary, and his internship at Interfaith Youth Core. The conversation tilts back and forth like that for a good part of the evening, and towards the end, one of the men thanks Chris for sharing his story, saying he has never actually met a homosexual before.

My story is nowhere near as brave or dramatic, but it was a small turning point in my life. I was in Seattle, passing through on a cross-country road trip the summer after I graduated from college, fully convinced that the world was sick and needed saving and that my righteous anger was the cure. In the Capitol Hill neighborhood, I saw an angry crowd gathered around an angry man reading angrily from the Bible and pointing dramatically to the ground. He kept repeating the words "Jesus" and "Hell" and the line "You are all going to hell." The crowd skipped the Jesus part and just basically told him to go to hell.

Normally, I would have jumped right in, tried to out-shout my fellow shouters. But for whatever reason, I just watched this time. And when the crowd had thinned out, I approached the man and asked, "Doesn't Jesus say to feed people?"

He looked a bit surprised. Probably he was so used to being met by anger that even a hint of something different sounded strange. Finally, he said, "Every morning my wife and I buy a loaf of bread and a dozen eggs and fix egg sandwiches for the homeless guys in the neighborhood."

"Oh," I said. "That's good." I started to walk away.

My back was still turned when I heard the man say: "Son, thank you for being decent to me."

That was it. It's a small memory but an important one for me, one that taught me that there is always the possibility to coax a bit of gentleness out of even the most belligerent situations. It is a memory that I am grateful this book helped me recover.

—◊—

There is a second memory that kept rolling through my mind as I read this, one that was brought back because the only response to a book as honest about life as this one is a bit of honesty with yourself. I remember the scene well. I am playing basketball with my friends. It is a beautiful day in the late spring of 1993. We are second-semester high school seniors in the suburbs of Chicago. We are on top of the world. I am joking about why I had chosen to room with my best friend from high school rather than roll the dice with the roommate lottery at the University of Illinois. The joke is this: "I don't want my assigned roommate to be a fag. What if he creeps up on me while I'm asleep?" Everybody laughs. I smirk a bit on the outside and feel a glow on the inside. It feels good to be the center of attention for even a fleeting moment.

It was one of many anti-gay statements I made growing up. For me, those statements didn't reflect a bigotry born of principle. They reflected a bigotry born of laziness and insecurity. I wasn't really afraid of getting assigned a gay roommate; I was afraid of getting assigned a roommate who didn't like me. Nerdy, skinny, brown-skinned, funny-name me. Getting to college and having my random roommate pick on me—that was a scene I could not countenance. And so I went the safest route, roomed with the kid I'd known since third grade, and scapegoated the cultural pariah I knew no one would defend. As I read about those years when Chris tortured himself because he was gay, I thought to myself, "I was one of the torturers."

I would like to think I am different now, that I have more compassion, more conviction, more courage. I would like to think that I at least try to identify common ground in the midst of conflict, that I am more likely to stand up for whomever the current cultural pariah is than seek a laugh at his expense. To the extent these things are true, I credit a single change in my life: becoming a more committed Muslim. Islam means to submit to the will of God, and I believe God is mercy and my Muslim-ness depends on whether I am merciful to those around me. Whatever compassion and conviction and courage I may have, I believe it comes from God.

This is a story that our culture's loudest atheists would scoff at. But when I shared it with Chris, he was eager to hear more. Whatever force or source strengthened and sustained my compassion, whether or not he believed in it, he wanted to affirm its presence in my life. That quality of listening and affirmation, of creating a space where, as Dorothy Day would say, it is easier for people to be good, that is Chris's gift, his grace note.

Those grace notes are woven through *Faitheist*. This is a book of light and music. Cherish the voice inside—smart, searing, playful, young and still emerging yet remarkably mature. Take a good look at the face on the cover, the one wearing that priceless "Is this really me? Holy cow, I'm so happy!" smile. It is the voice of someone nurturing a Humanism that seeks to build palaces of beauty and not just throw fits of rage. It is the smile of a man who will play an important role in American life and letters for years to come.

—EBOO PATEL
Founder and president,
Interfaith Youth Core

1

There's Nothing Worse Than a Faitheist

The chief deficiency I see in the skeptical movement is its polarization: Us vs. Them—the sense that we have a monopoly on the truth; that those other people who believe in all these stupid doctrines are morons; that if you're sensible, you'll listen to us; and if not, to hell with you. This is nonconstructive. It does not get our message across. It condemns us to permanent minority status.

—CARL SAGAN

I had never heard the word "faitheist" before, but I was pretty sure it wasn't a compliment.

I blushed and ran my hands through my short coffee-colored hair—a nervous habit—and cleared my throat, asking if it was intended to be an insult.

"Yes," he said without inflection. "There's nothing worse than a 'faitheist.'"

It was my first experience with the atheist movement, and for at least a moment I thought it might be my last. I'd been an atheist for a while, but I had hesitated to seek out a community of nonreligious people. I imagined that secular folks would be difficult to organize; that assembling atheists, agnostics, skeptics, freethinkers, and other nonreligious individuals would prove tricky because our common thread—that we are *not* something—underscores only what we do *not* believe. But as I progressed in my work as an interfaith activist, I noticed that one of the things that actually made people good at it was a groundedness in one's own identity. That, paired with my longing for a community of common belief, led me to begin searching for an organized community of nontheists.

The brusque brush-off occurred at a reception following a public discussion organized by a nonreligious group; the topic had been how the nonreligious—more specifically, atheists, agnostics, and other nontheistic, nonreligious people—should approach religion. I had suspected that there would be mixed feelings about religion. After all, I knew of the popular atheist discourse on the subject, which cast the religious not only as incorrect about metaphysical realities but as standing in the way of social and intellectual progress. But I had also hoped that someone might offer a more balanced perspective on religion, locating within the beliefs, desires, and actions of religious people similar values held by many nonreligious people.

I had gone with optimism and excitement. At the time, I was both an atheist and an intern for Interfaith Youth Core, an organization that helps mobilize young people to change the public narrative on religion from one of conflict to one of cooperation by engaging in dialogue around shared values and collaborative action. Because of my work, I felt I was in a particularly good position to discuss religion in the lives of nonreligious folks. I pictured myself saying with a well-meaning grin, "Hey, I work with religious people every day and my atheism is stronger than ever!" I hoped I might even serve as a bridge between two communities that are so often pitted against one another, to offer my insights as a nonreligious person working in an interfaith environment.

That aspiration was quickly curtailed. Throughout the program, religion—and religious people—were roundly mocked, decried, and denied. I'd arrived hoping to find a community bound by ethical and humanitarian ideals. Instead, I felt isolated and sorely discouraged.

Though I was disheartened by the event, I went to the post-panel reception, held at one of the panelists' apartments, because I hoped that if I spoke with more of the group members I'd find some people who shared my opinions or learn a bit more about why they believed differently than I did. Also, as a thrifty graduate student, free dinner and drinks were hard to pass up!

I walked in and instantly removed my shoes. The apartment was beautiful; the ceiling-to-floor windows allowed for a stunning view of Chicago's orange-and-white-lit skyline. The living room was impeccably clean. (I made a mental note to at least shove my dirty laundry in the closet when I got home.) I stood there and scanned the crowd; I was easily the youngest person there and un-fashionably underdressed (nothing new there). Looking down at my feet, I noticed there was a hole in each of my socks. *Maybe I should've left my shoes on*, I thought.

I sat down on the couch, carefully balancing a mint julep in one hand and a plate of hors d'oeuvres I couldn't name in the other, intensely aware of how out of place I must have seemed. Next to me on the couch were a woman in her mid-forties with a shimmer-ing peacock brooch and a man in his late thirties wearing a denim shirt and a tan corduroy vest. I introduced myself and asked what they'd thought of the panel. They raved: "Wasn't it wonderful how intelligent the panelists were and how wickedly they'd exposed the frauds of religion? Weren't they right that we must all focus our energy on bringing about the demise of religious myths?"

I paused, debating whether I should say anything. My "Min-nesota Nice" inclination warned me to let it be, but I had to say something. So I started small, asking them to consider that di-versity of thought and background fosters an environment where discourse thrives, where ideas are exchanged, and where we learn from one another.

I was stonewalled: "We have the superior perspective; everyone else is lost," said the woman with a flick of her hand that suggested she was swatting at an invisible mosquito. As a former Evangelical Christian, these words were hauntingly familiar, and they represented a kind of sure-handed certainty and dismissal—a kind of fundamentalist thinking, really—that I'd hoped to leave behind with my "born again" beliefs.

Our conversation continued, and I offered up petitions that the positive contributions of religious people be considered with equal weight alongside the negative.

"I understand what you're saying," I said, trying to weigh my words carefully, "but how can we discount the role religious beliefs played in motivating the Reverend Dr. Martin Luther King Jr. or Mahatma Gandhi?"

"Oh, I get it," the man jumped in with a sneer. "You're one of *those* atheists."

I wasn't sure what he meant, but it didn't sound like a good thing. I shifted my weight from one side to another—another nervous habit—and picked at an hors d'oeuvre that I thought might be some kind of cheese.

"What do you mean, 'one of *those* atheists?'"

"You're not a *real* atheist. We've got a name for people like you. You're a 'faitheist.'"

Not a *real* atheist. I'd heard words like that before—in my youth, when I was told I couldn't be a *real* Christian because I was gay. Once again I didn't fit the prescribed model, and I was not-so-gently shown the door.

Now, atheism is a bit different from Christianity in that atheism isn't a belief system. It's an identification marker that unifies a

minority of Americans who do not believe in God. But the impli-
cation was clear: you're at the wrong party, kid.

—⁓—

The next day, I attended my weekly religion class at Loyola University's Institute of Pastoral Studies, a Jesuit Catholic–run program for priests, nuns, and lay leaders. As the only self-identified
nonreligious person in the class, I was regularly met with many
questions. Once, a Catholic classmate cornered me in the eleva-
tor after class, proclaiming, "I've been dying to ask you about your
atheism!" Yet it never felt like an affront—she and the others were
genuinely (and understandably) curious.

Sitting in class the day after my botched attempt at seeking
secular community, I realized that I felt more at home with my
religious colleagues than with the atheists from the day before. I
looked around the room, focusing on each individual face; here
were people who believed in a God I had theorized away years ago,
yet they felt more like kin than most atheists I knew. While my
classmates felt that their religious beliefs were right, they not only
tolerated my beliefs but also enthusiastically embraced and challenged them.

Even though many parts of the United States remain incredibly segregated, we live in the most religiously diverse nation on
the planet, so one doesn't need to be an atheist enrolled in a Catholic institution to know that many American citizens are by default
required to coexist with people who believe radically different
things. The question I found myself asking that day, however, went
a step beyond that.

It was not, "Can religiously diverse people coexist in peace?"—
because, with some notable exceptions, Americans generally manage to tolerate one another's differences. It was, instead, "Can we

learn to seek out our commonalities instead of solely fixating on our differences?" This idea that it is worthwhile to make an intentional effort to find common ground is, to me, the difference between mere diversity and engaged pluralism. It is a question that our nation—in which a solid majority of Americans associate the extremists of 9/11 with all Muslims—is not close to resolving.[1]

The challenge of engaged religious diversity—of intersecting religious difference—is one that atheists know perhaps more intimately than most. In a nation full of believers of all stripes, we are, in a sense, outliers. This is perhaps why so many atheists today ask for equal airtime alongside our religious neighbors—we want to be taken seriously, to be seen as equally ethical individuals. The unfortunate side effect is that many atheists demand this at the expense of talking to our religious peers in a way that affords them dignity and respect.

Several years ago, Harvard Humanist chaplain Greg Epstein wrote a book called *Good Without God*, and his thesis was a simple but important one: our society must move beyond the question of *if* one can be good without God to *how* this may be accomplished. I join Greg in wanting people to move beyond wondering whether I am a moral individual, but I also join him in a companion call to our own community: atheism must move beyond defining itself—both in thought and in practice—in opposition to religion. If secular Americans want to be respected in our religiously diverse culture, we need to recognize that there is nuance and complexity in the diversity that defines it.

Ralph Waldo Emerson, a forefather of modern Humanism, is often said to have written these lines: "That which dominates our imaginations and our thoughts will determine our lives and character. Therefore, it behooves us to be careful what we worship, for what we are worshiping we are becoming."

Although some atheists—myself included—may cringe at the "w" word, Emerson reminds us to be wary of casting our neighbors in a negative light. Negative fixations will color our worldview. It's not always easy, but we must endeavor to live up to our best principles—just as we hope the religious will.

I have been speaking with secular communities about the idea of engaged religious pluralism for several years, and the results have been mixed. To my great surprise I am condemned and castigated by a subset of my fellow atheists on a regular basis, though most of the dismissals haven't been as clever as "faitheist"; "insufferable moron" comes to mind as a recent example, and it is one of the few that I would feel comfortable reproducing here. (If you're curious enough that you wish to know more, I trust you know how to use Google.) As I encourage my fellow atheists to respect and reach out to people who are religious, I am taken aback by how often I meet resistance and criticism.

Yet I didn't always feel this way. Once upon a time, I might've joined the groups of atheists decrying attempts to build intentional bridges of respect and collaboration between atheists and the religious. That interfaith cooperation is an important aspect of the quest to advance social progress wasn't a conclusion I came to overnight. In fact, after I stopped believing in God, I spent some time decrying the universal "evils of religion." I wanted nothing to do with the religious, and I was sure they wanted nothing to do with me.

—⁂—

Leaving my Loyola class the day after my first atheist event, I stepped out into the cool, windy Chicago afternoon and thought back to my conversation with the man who had called me a "faitheist." The bird-brooched woman had abandoned our discussion quickly, saying she didn't want to waste her time. The man and I had moved to the hall, grabbing more food and another drink on the way.

"Take Islam," he had said, leaning into a doorframe while I clutched my beer a little too tightly, the condensation running down my forearm to meet with the sweat that had just reached my elbow. "Now that's a violent faith. And don't try to tell me it's not, because I've read the Koran."

I thought of my friend Sayira, one of the most compassionate people I knew. Sayira was a young woman who was motivated by her Muslim faith to work for the economically disadvantaged. Sayira, who was close to receiving her black belt in karate. Sayira, one of the most gentle and loving people I'd ever met, repeatedly opened her home and her kitchen to anyone who was hungry. (And I am hungry a lot.) Sayira, a devout Muslim—and one of my role models. Sayira, who wasn't at all represented in this man's perception of Islam.

Clearing my mind of the conversation about Islam, I turned to face the overcast sky—the same direction I used to look up to in search of God—and recalled how once upon a time, in moments of contemplation such of this, I would direct a prayer up there. Years later, that notion felt alien, and so I looked to my feet to realize that I was standing in a puddle. (Waterproofing my Chuck Taylors hadn't done much to make up for the holes in their sides.)

I was not naïve then, nor am I now, to the atrocities committed in the name of religion around the world. I do not pretend that religion has not played a sizable role in a great many conflicts since people first began to conceive of it, or that it does not do so today. Historically, religion has been at the center of many atrocities—this is an undeniable, important fact. But I also know that at various points in history religion has been an enormous force for liberation. Religion has changed, reformed, and revolutionized the world, and it will continue to do so as long as it is central to the human story.

I didn't always understand that religion—both religious systems of belief and religious communities and individuals—is dynamic; I once spoke of it in the same static, flat, blanket terms that I hear many atheists use today. It was actively confronting my immobile conceptions of religion—by meeting and getting to know people like Sayira—that forced me to deconstruct my stereotypes. Stereotypes that are bolstered when prominent antitheists (individuals who are not merely nonreligious but outwardly antireligious—I'll return to this distinction later in this book) such as PZ Myers say things like, "Come on, Islam . . . It's bad enough to be the religion of hate, but to be the religion of cowardice ought to leave you feeling ashamed."[2] It is no wonder that many in the organized atheist community follow suit, lumping all religious believers together and shaming them as a uniformly condemnable bloc.

I fear that some atheists are doing what I used to do in my antireligious days: engaging in monologue instead of dialogue. After years of dismissing religious people outright, I realized that I was so busy talking that I wasn't listening. I was treating religion as a concept instead of talking to people who actually lived religious lives. When I started listening, something interesting happened: I saw that my approach to religion had been distorted. I'd been thinking narrowly about the texts, not about some of their positive applications; of the one-sided stereotypes, not the diverse spectrum of beliefs and practices. It was only after I observed the actual actions of religious communities—and, more importantly, engaged with religious people and their stories—that I was able to see the benefits of working across lines of religious difference.

Now I see interfaith engagement as the key to resolving the world's great religious problems—and they are many. I want the atheist community to join me, to share their stories and learn from those of the religious. And, most importantly, I want us to join with the religious in working to resolve the problems that afflict our world. Together, we will accomplish so much more than if we work alone or in opposition.

It took me some time to see this, and the years I spent alternately seeking a meaningful community and condemning religion en masse taught me a lot about why so many atheists struggle to approach the topic of religion with tact and grace. Being antireligious wasn't just a matter of opinion; it felt deeply personal. Before becoming strongly antireligious, I was a "born again" Christian struggling to reconcile the claims of that community with my same-sex attractions. And before that? I was nonreligious.

I've been on both sides of the divide and through my life experiences have developed some theories about why people of faith and nontheists struggle to relate to one another, and some ideas about how we might begin to bridge the divide.

I'd like to tell you my story because I think it matters. Certainly not more than any other story; we all have important stories to tell. I offer it up as a case study of sorts—an inside look into why one atheist struggled to find a healthy way to engage with the religious and why transcending our divisions is so important. In this time of polarization in nearly every area of public life, I want to share my story because I hope it will help build bridges at a time when we need more bridges than ever.

—⚬⚬—

When I first started as an intern at Interfaith Youth Core, I partnered with a group of young interfaith leaders to volunteer for a summer in a Chicago soup kitchen. All of us served together and followed each shift with a conversation on what motivates us to do interfaith community service work. I learned a good deal about

Catholic, Jewish, Muslim, and Protestant ethics, and I got to share my nonreligious notions of giving back to the community. In the process, I was able to engage with the calls to justice and empathy of my religious peers—and in doing so, my own social justice ethic matured. I still have a *lot* to discover, but I have already learned so much from people with stories that radically differ from my own.

Volunteering in that soup kitchen, I felt warm—and not just because I was standing over a hot food-serving line. (You can ask the students I work with if you want more examples of my terrible, cheesy sense of humor—I'll try to turn it off for the remainder of this book.) It was an entirely different feeling from the one I had gotten at the atheist panel on religion. Our actions were constructive; we had gathered to *build* something, not to tear something down.

I want to work to build a world where oppression and suffering can be eradicated. I realize this is already a *slightly* demanding task, and I believe that it is rendered impossible if I endeavor to do it alone or only alongside like-minded peers. I know that tackling the world's many problems requires the broadest possible network of resources, so if that requires me to work with people on areas of agreement while knowing we disagree on other issues, it is a promising start.

Still, there is a process of deconstruction involved in interfaith work—we must be willing to grapple with our fears and with the unknown, and uncover the hearts of diverse human experiences. I think about it like I did the Minnesota corn I grew up eating. We shuck to get to the part we can eat—the part that nourishes and feeds us—just as in interfaith work we try to get past our differences to look for shared aspirations: our common goodness. But those husks can be recycled and used, too: when I was younger, my mom taught my siblings and me to make dolls out of the husks that remained after we had cooked and consumed the sweet corn we bought at a roadside stand. Our differences don't need to be tossed aside; our diversity can be an asset instead of something to overcome. We can use our distinct skills and ideas to achieve our shared goals. The first step toward identifying them is sharing our stories with one another.

Sociologist Marshall Ganz writes, "Stories are what enable us to communicate [our] values to one another."[3] Psychologist Dan P. McAdams elaborates on this idea, suggesting that the values we exemplify through story move into action and vision: "Narrative guides behavior in every moment, and frames not only how we see the past but how we see ourselves in the future."[4]

What future will we imagine for ourselves and for the world? Is it a pessimistic narrative in which the religious and secular will continuously come into conflict until one triumphs over the other? Where religion is nothing more than a problem to be eradicated? In the words of IFYC founder and president Eboo Patel: Will we make of religion a "bomb of destruction, a barrier of division"—or can we make it "a bridge of cooperation"?[5]

Perhaps we can make the latter happen, if we listen to more stories and act—together—on the shared values they communicate.

—⁓—

Achieving a more cooperative world will require a dramatic change in how both atheists and the religious talk about atheism and religion. The problems of religious fundamentalism are apparent, and have already been responded to by many individuals far more qualified to do so than I. But what of atheism's antipluralism voices, like Sam Harris, who has said that "talk about the dangers of 'Islamophobia'" (discrimination or bias against Muslims or those who are perceived as being Muslim, which is a widely recognized, well-documented phenomenon in countries like the United States, United Kingdom, and Australia) is "deluded"?[6]

In a culture that increasingly asks us to check our religious and nonreligious identities at the door—to silence the values and stories we hold most dear—the "New Atheist" brand of secularism isn't helping. Although I believe that many New Atheist critiques of religion are correct and have helped many people find liberation from oppressive beliefs, some of these critiques have also often neglected to account for the full range of religious expression and have resulted in segregation that has parsed the religious and the secular into opposing camps. Religious and nonreligious identities are perhaps our most important social capital, for they signify our most central values, which inform how we act in the world. When we do not engage them, we lose out on something fundamentally important.

And people are resisting this enforced compartmentalization. For all of the gains we've made in the realm of scientific discovery, religiosity is still alive and well. Evangelicalism is thriving in many parts of the world, and fundamentalism is experiencing a radical surge. The 2010 Pew study on American Millennials—the generation born in the 1980s and 1990s—found that not only is "the intensity of [Millennials'] religious affiliation . . . as strong today as among previous generations when they were young," but that "levels of certainty of belief in God have increased" and that religious Millennials are "more inclined than their elders to believe their own religion is the one true path to eternal life."[7] Sociologists once predicted that religion would decline as a result of modernization, but precisely the opposite phenomenon has occurred. Some religious movements have remained steady while others have grown in recent decades, both in the United States and around the world, and sociologists have since retracted their predictions. According to Peter Berger, "Most sociologists of religion . . . [have] looked at the world and concluded that secularization theory—that is, the thesis that modernization necessarily leads to a decline of religion—does not fit the facts of the matter."[8] Psychologist David M. Wulff agrees: "At a point in human history when many thought that religion was on its way out, a casualty of science and rationality, we are witnessing a worldwide resurgence of fundamentalism, on the one hand, and a virtual explosion of interest in the 'new spirituality' on the other."[9]

With divisive religious fundamentalism on the rise, reactionary atheism that fixates on making antireligious proclamations is creating even more division. I believe that this so-called New Atheism—the kind that singles out the religious lives of others as its number one target—is toxic, misdirected, and wasteful. Disengaged or antagonistic atheism weakens our community's claim that an ethical life is possible without a belief in God, supplanting this with an alienating narrative that both distracts us from investing in community-building efforts of our own and prevents us from accomplishing anything outside of our small community. In addition, this militant, uncompromising antitheism inhibits people who do not believe in God from ever moving beyond articulating how they differ from the religious into the kinds of efforts that engender community building within and cooperation without. I do not believe it represents most atheists, but this perspective is currently the loudest and most visible one, speaking on behalf of atheists to the wider world and dictating the direction of the organized atheist community.

And so it is with this thought in mind that I begin to consider the lessons I have learned through my experiences. I'm going to do my best to tell my story honestly, but I haven't the best head for facts, names, dates, or anniversaries. (Ask my mom how many years she has received a Mother's Day card on time.) In other words, I'm a big-picture kind of guy; the details slip through the cracks in my floorboards.

Moreover, my mom swears up and down that several of the few vivid memories I've retained from childhood simply didn't happen. I'd like to believe she's wrong, but I fear she may be right. For example, she tells me that one day in community children's swimming lessons I earnestly informed all of my water-winged classmates that my mom had gotten pregnant with me when she was in high school; she turned to the parents standing alongside her at the side of the pool and explained, red-faced, that I suffered the deadly combination of being a wildly imaginative storyteller and having a shoddy memory. I'm not sure they believed her, but if there's one thing my mom is not, it's a liar—I just don't always get things right in hindsight.

Still, I will endeavor to tell it like it was. I may shift a few names or dates along the way to respect the privacy of some, but the spirit of what I write will be as true as I can muster.

The truth I aim to communicate is a simple and universal one: that all folks, whether Muslim or Christian or Hindu or atheist, deserve equal dignity. I hope my story will illuminate the problems that arise when we dehumanize people because of their atheism or religiosity, and when we resort to negative rhetoric and name-calling instead of seeking to understand our differences.

Just as I've personally reclaimed "queer" from those who have used it in an attempt to discount the legitimacy of my identity, I now reclaim "faitheist." If such a label insinuates that I am interested in both exploring godless ethics and identifying and engaging shared values with the religious—in putting "faith" in my fellow human beings and our shared potential to overcome the false dichotomies that keep us apart—then I am all for it.

To build a strong society, my Humanistic ethics encourage me to engage. This is much more than mere atheism, which is only a statement about what I don't believe in. After years of witnessing the ugliness that arises when rejection-based beliefs lead to the rejection of people, I now seek out ties that will bind us together.

After learning the necessity of engagement the hard way, I've uncovered an essential truth—the fellowship I had been seeking all along was already around me: a diverse community defined by shared values rather than shared identity.

2

Starting Secular,
Seeking Substance

*If you look deeply into the palm of your hand, you will see
your parents and all generations of your ancestors. All of
them are alive in this moment. Each is present in your body.
You are the continuation of each of these people.*

—Thich Nhat Hanh

"I come from a family where the only emotion respectable to show
is irritation. In some this tendency produces hives, in others literature, in me both."[1] Flannery O'Connor, a Catholic author whose
work has loomed over me ever since I first encountered it at sixteen (and for whom I have one tattoo and another planned), wrote
those words. They've always struck me as both funny and insight-
ful. My family, on the other hand, allowed for a much wider range
of emotional exposition—we're criers (sad, angry, and happy),
and we treat talking about our feelings like it's a sport. But, like
O'Connor, I know I must start with my family when considering
the ways in which I've been formed.

At its core, this book isn't about my family life; not directly,
anyway. It's about my experiences with religion. Religion was the
conductor of my adolescence and early adulthood, always standing before me, motioning vigorously while I struggled to discern
what I was being asked to do. It pulled, I followed; I pushed back, it

dodged out of the way. Like Isaac wrestling with God in the Book of Genesis, I scrapped with religion, demanded a blessing, and asked to be reinvented, newly named, and born again. Always trying to get a grip on the slippery questions of life, I was never quite sure what to do with conviction once I found it.

Although religion took the wheel, family was there first. And for something that has so thoroughly informed the second half of my still-short life, religion hardly factored into the first. In my youth, my religion was my family.

I was baptized in a United Methodist church, but as I understand it the ceremony wasn't an especially pious affair. In fact, I'm told the most notable thing about it was that my spirited twenty-month-old sister ran to the front and lifted up the minister's heavy, creased robes right as he proclaimed: "Let the little children come unto me, and do not hinder them." It would be some time before any of us entered a church again.

Any theological commitments my parents might have made that day were realized solely on a practical level: I was indoctrinated into a commitment to fairness and an ethos of love and justice, and I was carefully watched over—not by God but by devoted humans. I had no idea what sin meant, but I did experience the heat of shame whenever my mom cast a disappointed eye my way in response to bad behavior. I learned the merits of community from sharing limited resources with three siblings close in age—the mileage we made together taught me more than any other community I've belonged to since.

I knew religion existed, but it was something other people did. As far as I could tell it was actually something of a luxury; *other* people could afford to sit in pews on Sunday morning and attend coffee hour, following one ritual with another. Those people had all the time in the world for singing and donuts and chit-chat about Bobby's soccer practice and Nancy's spelling bee.

But not us, no—we have a work ethic, I would tell myself with a self-congratulatory sense of pride as we scrubbed the floors while "Ring of Fire" scratched from the record player. On a Sunday when we had no chores, we'd head to the free zoo in St. Paul to mimic the monkey's squeals or to a shadowy, densely wooded Minnesota State Park, taking advantage of the quiet that would disappear as post-church crowds descended later in the day. If we did have chores, after cleaning, mom would take us to the grocery store to get the cheap Sunday specials before the afternoon post-church crowds took over; we'd nibble on free samples of frozen pizza and blueberry yogurt in place of lunch. My mom prided herself on finding the big coupon item for each of the three major grocery stores in our town—the *really* cheap item intended to get you in the door so that you would buy other things once there—and planned our meals around them. She made it into a game for us, like a scavenger hunt—we'd shriek with excitement when we used the coupon at Jubilee Foods that got us a dozen eggs for 99 cents plus a free gallon of Minute Maid orange juice. We took pleasure in finding the best beef roast before it was picked over and taking it home to cook a simple but delicious Sunday dinner. After dinner, our bellies full, we'd take an afternoon nap listening to the record player spin the story of *Winnie the Pooh and the Blustery Day.*

My childhood was marked by simplicity and hard work and love—which is to say that it was actually quite carefree. My mother did a good job of instilling in us a deep sense of gratitude for the things we had; I didn't really notice that we had less than other people until I was older and began to look for differences everywhere. It never seemed odd to me that we wore hand-me-down and homespun clothing, or that we used homemade remedies like covering our hair with mayonnaise and saran wrap when we got lice from someone at school. When we were young children my mom made sure my siblings and I were well cared for—it was only later in life that I started telling myself that my story was that of "the poor kid." The life she provided was rich, filled with complex colors of every hue, with trips to the beach in the early hours of the day before the parks became overcrowded with people desperate to escape the summer swelter, with arts and crafts and makeshift blanket forts.

Her inventiveness masked the meagerness we lived with; I never even realized until later in life that during my youngest years she had only owned two pairs of jeans and a few sweatshirts. She had an unparalleled aptitude for spinning straw into gold—our Christmases were full of hand-crafted and recycled gifts, and for birthdays she would set up elaborate party games, hanging pretzels from the ceiling with ribbon, hand-painting a bunny for cotton ball pin-the-tail-on-the-rabbit, and writing up thought-provoking trivia. My earliest years were characterized by imaginative games my siblings and I invented such as "Mean Diseased Cat," where we manned our alert stations in anticipation of the return of a particularly feral cat that once meandered down our street; by the birthday cakes my mom painstakingly prepared; by the hand-crafted skip-its, teeter-totters, and pajamas that were our most prized possessions; by sitting down together as a family for dinner every single night, even if it was just bottom-shelf macaroni and cheese or saltine crackers topped with melted Kraft Singles, which we ate near the end of particularly tight months. I didn't realize that you could buy Play-Doh at the store until I was nearly in middle school; we always made ours from scratch. I think we enjoyed it more that way, having concocted it ourselves before using it to build new things. We were deeply invested in everything we did, because most things were an act of creation and an act of love.

—␣—

Perhaps the only absence I felt was that of my mother's mother, my Grandma Judith. I don't remember much about her, but it was always clear to me that she had had a significant influence on the family. For much of my childhood, I heard comments comparing the two of us—how my face bore a striking resemblance to hers, how I was sensitive like her, how she would have appreciated the poem I wrote in first grade comparing the clouds to popcorn and the sun to the old-fashioned spinning popcorn popper we owned. My favorite Christmas ornament was one that she had given me; I gingerly wrapped it in toilet paper and put it away every year, careful not to break it.

Though Grandma Judith died when I was young, I was immersed in tales of who she was. My mother would tell us stories when one of us was hospitalized, while we waited for the free Dayton's department store Christmas display to open, when we were stuck in our non-air-conditioned car for a long and sticky summer drive, or even while sitting at the dinner table. We were trained to cherish stories from the start, and a good number of them were about my Grandma Judith.

Judith was an eccentric and intensely compassionate woman. She was, in many ways, ahead of her time. In the 1980s she developed a curriculum on human sexuality for a quiet Minnesota Methodist congregation's confirmation class that would be considered controversial by many churches even today. But though she called herself a Christian, she was deeply fascinated by world religions, created astrology charts for all of her grandchildren, and visited psychics regularly. She thought herself an openly spiritual woman, but she was quite serious about her convictions—after reading *The Omen*, she threw it in the fire, saying she didn't want evil in her house. But at the end of the day, her Methodist church was her home; though she didn't agree with everything it taught, she thought that the church provided a lot of good things.

My grandma raised her children to be nonjudgmental, so my mom didn't think anything of it when she went to her mother's for dinner in 1986 and was greeted by three HIV-positive gay men. At that time, people with HIV/AIDS were still taboo for many—especially in Minnesota—but, my mother said, it was exactly like Judith to welcome into her home those whom mainstream society rejected. This attitude of openness was instilled in my mother at a young age, and my siblings and I were raised to wear gender-neutral clothing, to play with non-gendered toys, and to think of ourselves as unrestrained by societal norms. My mother gave dolls to all three of her boys so that we might learn to be nurturing and caring; my younger brother Colton, who would go on to play football and head up his college's rugby fraternity, loved his doll more than any of us did, making blankets for it and taking it with him everywhere. My mother credits her nonconformist, outside-the-box parenting to Judith.

My sister was born in September of 1985, and my mother describes that time as idyllic; my mom was young, her mother was young, and it seemed as if everything would continue on forever. However, a year later—when my mother was eight weeks pregnant with me, vomiting every morning with sickness—Judith was diagnosed with cancer, and that vision changed dramatically.

Still, people were optimistic. Judith was young, and if anyone could beat the odds, she could. She was a leader in the community, someone who lived fully and forcefully. She was liked and respected by everyone who knew her. Though my mom recalls her as being "like the old witch in the house on the corner in a conservative community," Judith worked with lots of different people. Because of her spirit of openness and her efforts to build bridges with everyone, she was admired and loved—if not fully understood—by most. She threw her entire self into her many projects and always came out on top; so it would be—would *have* to be—with her cancer treatment.

Because my aunts and uncles were all off at college or still in high school when Judith was diagnosed, my mother became

Judith's primary caretaker. My father was always working, so it was often just my mom, my sister, Judith, and me at the house. Everyone was optimistic—Judith lived a healthy lifestyle, had a chemotherapy regimen, and, in the summer of 1987, realized a lifelong dream of going to Europe. But shortly after she returned, so did her cancer. Thinking it was localized, the doctors performed radiation. But in the fall of 1988, her cancer came back again—this time, in the bones of her neck. They continued treatment, and everyone remained cautiously optimistic about her odds.

Such optimism wouldn't last long. While teaching a world religions class at a local community college the next year, Judith thought she'd hurt her back. She had a CAT scan that revealed a tumor in her spine. By January of 1990, the doctors said there was nothing more that could be done. Judith was moved home for hospice care. Knowing she had some life insurance, she treated us to shrimp from Red Lobster and told us stories from her childhood, like how she'd purposefully get dirt on her dresses so she wouldn't have to wear them and how her favorite picture of herself was one where she was dressed in her cowboy costume, her face in a serious grimace, a toy gun in her hand. She told us these stories from behind an eye patch, which she had to wear because of her brain tumor. She had personalized it by sewing a crystal onto it—she wanted to sparkle—and we giggled and told her she looked like a pirate. "I got this crystal from the buried treasure I dug up," she said in a mischievous whisper, and we believed her.

For much of her battle with cancer, Judith had felt she owed it to people to get better. Her life had been defined by how she had taken care of things, how she had triumphed and beaten all of the odds; so, of course, it would be the same in this fight. She had so many plans still unrealized—but by the time she was in the last few months of her life, she had accepted her impending death. When she was told nothing more could be done, the pressure to be perfect was lifted, and she adopted a relieved air. My mom recalls her saying to a friend: "I would prefer to stay—but if I have to go, I'm kind of excited to see what's next."

Judith felt calm and at peace. With this in mind, we planned a trip to California to visit my father's brother and his family. It would be my first time leaving Minnesota. Because we would be in California during my birthday, Judith insisted on hosting a party for me the day before we left. She seemed more alive than she ever had. The light from the birthday candles reflected off her bejeweled eye patch as she sang "Happy Birthday" to me. I clapped my pudgy hands, smudged with green frosting, and tried to join her in song. Death seemed far off for all of us; I never could have imagined that this would be our final moment together.

Several days later, we arrived in California to my aunt and uncle standing in the driveway. Meeting us at the car, they told my mother that Judith had died the day before. It was the first time we had been away from her since her diagnosis, and it was something of a surprise; she had been doing so well but had apparently taken a dramatic turn for the worse shortly after we left. Her breathing became short and labored the night she died, and she began talking aloud to her deceased father, who had meant a lot to her. She drifted in and out of coherence, her chest rising and falling with sharp inhalations. In the middle of the night, while everyone else was asleep, she had removed her own oxygen mask.

"She died," my mom said, turning to face us, her eyes glistening as the California sunlight caught in the beads of water materializing there like drops of dew stuck in a spider's web.

I didn't understand. I could hear waves crashing upon the Pacific shoreline less than a mile away; I had already enthusiastically excavated my swimsuit from my bag. I had never seen an ocean before, but I knew it would be big, blue, and expansive—something that went out and out forever.

"Died?" I asked, looking from my mom to my sister, who seemed to know what my mom was saying. "What is 'died'?"

"It means your Grandma Judith is no longer with us," she said, reaching out to touch my arm.

"Well I know that," I exclaimed, excited to have solved the riddle. "She's back home in Minnesota!"

The waves kept rolling into shore out of sight as my mom picked me up and carried me inside. I still didn't really understand what death was, but I knew I was loved.

Following Grandma Judith's death, we wrote her letters and left them scattered around the house, almost like leaving cookies for Santa, placed with care at dusk, hoping they'd be gone by morning. We would scribble in crayon questions like, "Do you have a cat in heaven? Are there unicorns there? Are you happy? Do you miss us?" We'd also fill her in on our lives, though we suspected she already knew, given her heavenly vantage: "I wrote a poem that got published in a magazine! We got a wiener dog! Sorry Grandma, but we have to sell your house." My mother was honest with us that Grandma Judith was gone but wanted her to still be a part of our lives, and so she humored our letter writing. For the first few years after Grandma died, my mom would set a place at the table for her at Christmas, an empty plate and chair that symbolized far more than the twinkling lights on our tree did. We came to think of her as a special person watching over us, though we never talked about what that meant theologically. I grew up thinking all dogs go to heaven, and all people, too.

Though there were supernatural aspects to this—the idea that she was in heaven, or that we might see her again someday—it was benign. The emphasis was on carrying her forward into our lives, in seeing her live on in our memories and in the stories we told about her and about how much we loved her. We weren't taught to see death as a bad thing; we discussed it very openly. Grandma

Judith had even given my sister a special wand, saying, "If you want to talk to me, use this." I'm not sure we actually believed that we could talk to her, but it was nice to think of her as still being with us in some way.

Looking back on her life and my memories of her, it's clear that my grandma deeply informed the person I've become. I didn't learn until I was an adult that she had dedicated the final years of her life to interfaith and queer activism—she was even a founding member of the AIDS Interfaith Council of the Twin Cities. Maybe she was just looking to project her interests on someone, but she hinted to my mother that I might be gay and declared that my astrology chart made it clear that my life would rotate around religion. I don't give astrology credence, but I feel like she'd be pleased that her predictions panned out.

Her diagnosis and death changed everything—my mom looks back at it now as one of the most defining events of her life, a shift that completely altered how she parented. My mom, in her early twenties at the time, became more interested in living in the moment and in cultivating that attitude in her children—but also in ensuring that we maintained a connection to our past. Storytelling became a central part of how we communicated with one another.

Because of this understanding, my childhood was exceptionally full. Yet as I got older, I began to see that others approached things differently. And, before long, I started to wonder if "differently" actually meant "better." Especially in regard to religion.

—⋙—

As a young adult, I fell in love with the music of a band called of Montreal. One of my favorite of Montreal songs is "Gronlandic Edit," in which lead singer Kevin Barnes muses about how, while it might be nice to believe in a god, he is unsure of which god to choose.

That song stirred a sense of internal recognition the first time I heard it because, like many young Americans today, I was not passed down a god to believe in.

Perhaps because of this noted absence—and because of the shadow of my grandmother, a woman who appreciated religious questions more than anyone—I was a peculiar child. My first-grade teacher, who encouraged me to pursue my love of poetry and self-publish a collection I titled *Popcorn, Ducks, and Pink Lemonade*, has told me that it just never occurred to me to be hesitant in my curiosity.

My mother describes me similarly: as an unapologetically inquisitive child with a perpetually sunny disposition. Even as a baby I wasn't very fussy—I was always affable, naturally in a good mood. But because of my perpetual cheer I was perhaps a bit naïve and often missed social cues. The summer before sixth grade, I visited the middle school I'd be attending in the fall and walked directly up to the principal, shaking his hand and stating very matter-of-factly: "Hi. I'm Christopher Delos Stedman, and I'll be attending school here next year." It didn't strike me that this might be an odd thing for an eleven year old to do.

In our family, being different was sometimes seen as a badge of honor. I remember my mother giving my sister advice after a group of popular girls made fun of her: "Casi—you don't want to look and be just like everyone else. Being popular, with the same clothes as everyone else . . . who would want that? You're not like other people, and that sets you apart." My sister smiled and turned toward me, and we exchanged knowing looks. We knew our mother was just trying to make us feel better about being different, but we didn't want to admit that it worked.

Even so, I was mostly oblivious to the fact that I was a bit odd for much of my childhood. It only occurred to me in obvious ways, like when I sat in my desk red-faced as they announced my top-five finish in the Minnesota Geography Bee over the school loudspeaker. Sure, I liked geography and that was a little weird, but everyone had peculiar interests. Unlike later in life, my differences didn't define me.

My mom knew I didn't quite fit in; when she would go to parent-teacher conferences, she'd prepare to hear from teachers that I was nontraditional. But instead, they would usually say: "He doesn't socialize like most kids—he doesn't have a core group of close friends—but he's very happy and gets along fine with most students. He's a little bit of a misfit, but it seems like he's found a way to deal with it . . . or, perhaps, just doesn't really recognize it."

Still, when I was informed the summer after second grade that we were moving, I was less than thrilled. For as long as I could remember we had lived in a stucco one-level lump, with a living room, a kitchen, and three bedrooms for six of us—my mother and father in one room, my sister in another, and my two brothers and me in the third. My mom had spruced up our confined quarters by hand-painting fantastical environments around us; the walls of the room I shared with my brothers were covered in brush-stroked meandering vines and acrylic animals. These flourishes were a manifestation of the way in which we were encouraged to imagine a more expansive world than the one we saw around us. After bed-time I'd read atlases, the pages illuminated by a nightlight hooked into a thin brown extension cord, and it was as if the tropical bird perched on a giant leaf behind my bed fluttered in the shadows cast with the turning of each page, chirping of the infinite possibility contained within each new nation.

But our new house was unlike the one we'd occupied before: it had two levels, a dining room, and even a deck. Our backyard faded into a marsh, and wild deer, geese, and turkey regularly emerged from the thicket like magic. I even had my own bedroom! So though I missed our old house, it didn't take long for me to get used to the change.

The new neighborhood, too, was idyllic. Within a block's walk was a quaint apple orchard, owned and operated by a woman who always gave me a free apple when I walked my dog, Rosi, up to visit. The family next door, who had moved from Mexico about ten years prior, invited me over to practice my Spanish; the couple across the street paid me to feed their cats when they were out of town. A boy my age lived a block away, and he had a Nintendo 64 that he let me use. It felt like a real community.

We were living the American dream—moving on up, economically and socially. Before our move, my wardrobe mostly consisted of clothing donated by family friends or hand-sewn sweatshirts. Before my first day of third grade, I was taken to the store and allowed to buy a few brand-new, never-before-worn items of clothing. I sported them proudly, favoring them among the other well-worn items in my wardrobe.

Making new friends was easier than I had imagined it would be, too. The same month we moved, another third-grader moved in a couple houses up the road. I'd pass her house while walking my dog and she'd come out with hers. They'd play together, and so would we.

Her name was Lia, and we gravitated toward one another immediately. She was adopted from South Korea into an interfaith family: her mother was a Jew, her father a Catholic. Our friendship was my first exposure to religion. Lia celebrated Hanukkah and Christmas, Passover and Easter, and maintained practices from both traditions as well as cultural practices that invoked her Korean heritage. Lia's parents were committed to her engagement with her religious and cultural histories.

My family celebrated Christmas and Easter—but as strictly secular affairs. We saw Jesus as a good guy who did good things, but there was no discussion about God or salvation, and we didn't go to church, even on those holidays. In fact, I never heard the word "God" in my house as a child. But I didn't hear the word "atheist" either; we weren't for or against religion, we were just without it—irreligious.

I never viewed our lack of religious belief or participation as a deficit in my life, but as my friendship with Lia developed, I became jealous of the sense of connection she got from her traditions and started to wonder if my life—in spite of my tight-knit family's practices and ethics—was a bit empty in comparison.

Through our friendship, I began to wonder what my life would look like were I Jewish. How would my life have been different if I had been raised in a community like that? What was I missing out on?

I decided to find out. When Lia invited me to join her family for a Seder celebration, I replied with an enthusiastic yes. I started to imagine myself converting to Judaism: I'd wear a yarmulke or kippah and attend Shabbat services every Friday. I'd speak fluent Hebrew and have a bar mitzvah. It all seemed so exciting and foreign and enriching.

Finally, it was time to try it out. I paced my house all day, waiting to go over to Lia's. After what felt like forever, I walked up the street, was let in by Lia's mother, and took a seat, my heart racing. Sitting at the table with Lia's family for a Seder celebration, I listened intently to the story of Passover, to the prayers, taking in the unfamiliar rituals with wide eyes.

"Baruch atah Adonai Eloheinu Melech ha-olam . . ."

Surrounded by roasted lamb bone, bitter herbs and eggs, parsley, drawn blinds, and someone else's family, I listened as a group of mostly strangers recited what was, to me, pure gibberish. Their words sounded funny, forced, and entirely alien. I looked over at Lia and tried to make eye contact, but hers were squeezed shut, her head bowed.

It was all very interesting—a kind of weird, mystical demonstration; something I could observe as an astonished third party but didn't really comprehend—but, somehow, even in the rush and thrill of first exposure, I knew I didn't belong there.

As I sat there, plate and meal before me, I did my best to conjure up an image of myself in this story—but, to my great surprise, I could not.

In that moment I became conscious that though this was a beautiful story that enriched my life, it was not *my* story. I had not been handed a religious tradition from on high containing stories that began with the creation of the world—and that was okay. My lot was to be a collector, compiling stories of family and friendship, crafting my own tradition in community with others. My family had already begun this process for me, providing stories of generations past, instilling morals and practices of sharing and love and humor, and those I love continue to inform it. I was already fulfilled by family; I wasn't lacking anything. With this realization, I ran home and gave my mom a giant hug.

"Being Jewish seems fun," I said. "But I like being me just fine."

I wish I had held on to that lesson as I transitioned into adolescence, but as I started to see the world as it truly is, the confidence that defined my youth began to fade.

—⁓—

Like most children, my attention span was short, and so my interest in Judaism had been extremely ephemeral. I kept the children's *Teach Yourself Hebrew* book I'd gotten, but it became an artifact of a fleeting interest, housed in a box alongside other short-lived hobbies like Pogs and Pokémon and Star Wars trading cards.

The next year, as I started the fourth grade, my family flirted with Unitarian Universalism. We began attending a family friend's church about thirty minutes away from our house. The church was vibrant and offered its congregants a lot by way of moral guidance and communal support, and I enjoyed Sunday school for the friends I made and the fun games we played. But one Sunday, I was caught off guard.

"Please join me in extending a warm welcome to our speaker this week, kids," the Sunday school leader said, surrounded by colorful construction paper cutouts of snowflakes. "This is Linda. She's going to talk to us about being a lesbian!"

I bit my tongue and tried not to giggle, looking around to see if anyone else was attempting to stifle a laugh, too. I had heard that word before and, though I didn't know exactly what it meant, I knew being a lesbian was something that was supposed to be funny to the rest of us. Other kids at school would laugh when they heard the word, or employ it as an insult. But here was someone wearing the word like it was a fancy hat or a nice blazer—an important adornment, something to be proud of.

A year prior, a relative who lived in the South had come to stay with us for a week. I vaguely recall my mother saying something about her being a lesbian, but I was mostly interested in the fact that she had hairy legs, rode a motorcycle, and loved strong, dark black licorice, which I thought tasted vile.

But now, a year later, it struck me as notable. Funny, even. I began to chuckle a little—quietly—which caught the attention of the Sunday school leader. She shot me an angry look, and I quickly sat up straight and wiped the smirk from my face.

Huh, I thought. *A lesbian. That's funny, right?*

I looked around and saw a sea of straight-faced and attentive kids facing forward.

So why isn't anyone laughing?

I continued to ruminate on this curiosity after she finished speaking, and I soon discovered that I was not alone in doing so. During the drive home, peering up at the trees shadowing the winding country road, my sister asked my mom how she would know if she was a lesbian herself.

My mom laughed and said, "You'd just know."

Unsatisfied by this answer, my sister and I decided it would be a fun joke to convince my mom that my sister was a lesbian. Piling onto a big white chair in our parents' room, we murmured schemes of how best to get a rise out of Mom.

"I think we should tell her that I'm a lesbian," Casi said.

"Do you think she'll believe you?!" I gasped.

"Of course she will!" my sister said, and we laughed. My sister was the outlaw troublemaker of the family, and I was often her unwitting accomplice. As a young child, she'd wake me before dawn with a pair of toenail clippers to give me a haircut, or a snack we weren't supposed to eat. She was my big sister, so I usually didn't question her logic.

Satisfied by our plan, we ran to the living room, where my mom sat reading a book.

"Mom," Casi said, deadpan. "I think I'm a lesbian." We mashed our hands into our pockets, silently gleeful, awaiting an outburst.

"That's great," my mom replied, equally deadpan, aware that this wasn't a serious admission. "Have you cleaned your room yet?"

It was totally anticlimactic, and we were disappointed that Mom didn't take the bait. Years later, Casi would learn that I was gay after making fun of me for buying an issue of *Rolling Stone* featuring a shirtless Justin Timberlake on the cover, and we would recall this incident, laughing through our tears and her apologies.

My mom, who had been raised in such a tolerant and open environment, didn't really sit us down to "have the talk" on these things, assuming we'd absorb the same kind of open-mindedness she grew up with. But, as she and I have discussed in adulthood, she took for granted that kids get messages—often ones that are not great—from places other than their parents.

At that time, I never bothered to ask myself if I might be gay. As a fourth grader, it just didn't occur to me. Maybe it was my naiveté, but I was also preoccupied by other differences. I was beginning to realize that Shoreview wasn't as idyllic as I'd first thought. It was very different from Coon Rapids, the town we had lived in before—social and economic disparities were harsher, the lines thicker, the "in group" mentality more noticeable.

Because I was a bit of an oddball, and because we didn't have the kind of money many others at my school did, I gravitated toward other outsiders. My group of friends was an eclectic bunch, consisting of the kids who didn't quite fit in.

I began to notice that my black friends—significantly in the minority at my school—were sometimes treated differently than my other friends. Then, in fifth grade, I read Alex Haley's *Roots*. I checked out the unabridged version from the library and bragged to my mom that I was about to read the biggest book I had ever seen.

I was quickly humbled. I remember vividly how I sat on my bed and sobbed when Kizzy was taken away from her family. I was mortified that something so horrific, so inhumane, could happen—let alone in my own country's recent history. That such injustice could exist in the world at all, and that it would go so largely unchallenged, ripped open a hole in my gut that exists to this day.

I was just a kid; I had no framework for responding to this disequilibrium. Slavery had been addressed in my history classes, but it was skirted around, treated as historical fact and not human experience. *Roots* provided so much new information—but, all the more, it put the stories of real *people* on these historical events. I imagined my black friends going through what the characters in *Roots* experienced and felt ill.

After *Roots,* I began to tear through other books that documented and humanized real-world tragedy. *The Diary of Anne Frank* brought tears to my eyes; *Hiroshima* made me feel nauseous. I cried through each one and wondered what was wrong with some people that they could commit such atrocities. I couldn't believe that my country had perpetuated slavery, waited so long to respond to the Holocaust, dropped atomic bombs on Japan, and taken the land and lives of the people who had lived in America first.

I was filled with so much concern for the world, and such a desire for justice, that I needed an outlet. For the first time in my life, I began to care as much about the well-being of others as I did about my own desires, and I wanted to do something to help people.

We had stopped going to the Unitarian Universalist church—they'd been too far away for us to continue going regularly—so it was just a matter of time before I found another moral outlet.

Soon, I'd learn what it meant to be a part of a despised minority. But first, I had to lose my family and find God.

3

Conversion and Confusion

Hateful to me as are the gates of hell,
Is he who, hiding one thing in his heart,
Utters another.

—HOMER

Middle school was a time of great change. It started with my school schedule; instead of spending all hours in the same room with the same people, we moved from classroom to classroom throughout the day. It made me feel like an adult—such freedom! Between classes, there was even time to have conversations with friends I ran into on the way from one side of the school to the other.

One day I was on my way from English to math when I bumped into a group of people I idolized. They were more popular than I was. They donned brand-new, name-brand clothes every fall, as opposed to the out-of-fashion, worn-out clothing I wore year after year. I had classes with some of them, and they were always friendly to me, though it was clear that they were in a different social class than I was. We started talking, and after a few minutes one of them piped up about how I should think about checking out the Christian youth group they all went to. He said that it was a lot of fun—not boring, like his parents' church—and that there was even free pizza. I wanted to become good friends with this group, and pizza for free sounded almost too good to be true. A friend who lived nearby said her mom could give us a ride, and so I decided to go.

My first Christian worship experience was a revelation. The youth center, a converted office building, buzzed with energy. Social barriers were eradicated for a few hours—popular kids mingled with nerds unflinchingly. After thirty minutes of conversation in the foyer, people began to trickle into the largest room. A projector displayed a welcome message on a screen at the front, with microphones and musical instruments littered across the stage beneath. A man with a dollop of wispy flaxen hair and baggy cargo pants welcomed everyone before leading the crowd in a game called, "Honey, if you love me, will you please smile?" The goal of the game was simple: don't laugh. Though feeling a bit timid, I jumped right into it, having so much fun I was unable to contain my laughter—which meant I was out of the competition almost immediately.

When the game was finished, we all sat down and a group of young people joined the man at the front and played a few worship songs, fronted by a "worship leader" with long brown hair and a bright orange guitar plastered with Bible-verse bumper stickers. After the music, the pastor preached about Jesus—I'd heard about Him but didn't know all that much, besides the fact that many people I knew claimed to love Him—and then asked everyone to split into small groups. Because it was my first time, I stayed in the main room and talked with the worship leader about my interests and why I had come to church that night. However, my attention was focused on a guy standing in the hall, just outside the room—my "welcomer."

As a first-timer, I had been assigned a welcomer when I walked in the door. He was a handsome young man in his late teens with closely cropped hair and a fitted "Jesus Saves" t-shirt that clung to his athletic build. Escorting me around the room, he flashed a smile of brilliant, perfectly aligned teeth every time he introduced me to someone. He had put his hand on my back to guide me through the crowd and the touch was electric; later, when he gave me a hug goodbye, I decided I'd definitely come back the next week.

He wasn't there a week later, but in his place was an entire community of people who not only remembered meeting me the week before but expressed sincere joy at my return. I was disappointed that my welcomer was absent, but I felt enveloped by love.

My third time there, I took the big leap. In the middle of worship, the youth minister asked if anyone wanted to come forward to commit themselves to Christ and accept Him into his or her heart. He looked me square in the eyes, and a couple of people standing near me, knowing I was new to church, turned and looked out of the corner of their eyes to see if I was going to go forward. I caught the eye of my welcomer, back once again, and he flashed that brilliant smile and nodded approvingly. I turned left and locked eyes with one of the popular girls who invited me to come a few weeks before; she was beaming. I took a first step toward the front of the room, and she broke into a euphoric grin.

I was consumed by a sea of people with heaven-bound hands, their eyes full of adoration for the guitar-carrying man on stage who, from his gentle doe eyes to his scraggly brown beard and flowing hair, served as stock-image white Jesus placeholder. Ushered forward by friendly slaps on my back and the thrill of spiritual symbiosis set to music, I joined the copastors on stage.

I wanted to do this. I liked church, I liked the people there, but even more so, I just wanted to be a part of it all. I wanted to be a part of the Christ club. I wanted a relationship with Jesus. I wanted a place to belong, and I wanted a framework for making sense of injustice and suffering. The pastor preached about a loving and forgiving God who would always care for me and who would provide those things.

Standing at the front of the room beneath bright, colored lights, I echoed the words of the youth pastor—"Jesus, I believe you came and died on the cross for my sins and I accept you as my Lord and Savior; please come into my heart"—and became a Christian.

Accepting Christ into my heart felt immense. I was affirmed by the community but, incredibly, I also felt a foreign sensation—an inner warmth, like how I felt when my mom told me she was proud of me, but different, bigger. In that moment I was sure that I *felt* Jesus take up residence in my heart.

It was as if my entire world changed in a single moment. I suddenly had a companion—and an accompanying community—that would never leave my side. I was captivated by the idea of a love that was undeserved, unending, and guaranteed—just as the other certain source of love in my life began to change dramatically.

—⚬⚬—

As a child, I had been optimistic and cheerful; I didn't see the darker side of things. So when my parents told us they were getting divorced, I was blindsided. My sister bragged that she had seen it coming—that she had noticed the awkward silences, the new sleeping arrangements, and the fact that my mom had stopped wearing her wedding ring—but I hadn't. I was devastated.

To make matters worse, my father began acquiring and losing jobs with increasing frequency. His inability to hold a job enabled him to avoid his mandatory child-support payments, and my mother went from being a homemaker to working multiple jobs while studying to get her insurance license, including waiting tables at a diner. (She always returned home from a shift with one of our favorite sandwiches, cutting it into fourths as my siblings and I clamored to tell her about how our days had gone. We hardly ever asked about hers.) Money had been scarce before, but love had always been in abundance. Abruptly, both were now in doubt.

As my father faded from view and my mother scrambled to keep our family together, I felt rootless and, for the first time, without a community. Jesus and His followers fixed that, and my mom's home-cooked meals were replaced by greasy pizza and communion wafers.

Though pizza and popularity brought me in and the love of Christ and community kept me, it was in fact the image of Christ as a social reformer that impacted me most. Like the popular kids welcoming nerds like me into their community, Christ had transcended the social barriers of his time, serving the poor and needy, healing lepers and hanging out with social outcasts. The radical nature of Christ as someone who tore apart the fabric of the social structures of His time rattled me in the best way possible; it got me thinking about my own place in the world and what I could do to make a difference in the face of the horrific inequalities I'd read about in *Roots*, *The Diary of Anne Frank*, and *Hiroshima* the year before.

Exploring the justice-oriented aspects of Christianity required investigation on my part, as the church community I quickly became a part of did not trumpet them. Service work was not a big part of my faith life at first—we were too busy playing games and singing worship songs to do much else—but I ended up going on service trips with YouthWorks (an organization that provides such opportunities for Christian youth) to paint houses on the Pine Ridge American Indian Reservation in South Dakota, to volunteer at a nursing home in Duluth, Minnesota, and to install insulation in homes in rural Kentucky. I felt like I was putting my faith into action.

That I stumbled onto the image of Jesus as a reformer and agent of social change was no accident—after my third time at church, I asked my Grandma Kay to buy me a *Teen Study Bible*, which I read fervently. I was asking a lot of questions, and in the process I discovered two things almost simultaneously: I was queer, and my church would kick me out if they discovered my secret.

What an awful irony. Mere months after converting, I was finally able to put words to something I had known all along but couldn't name. I still remember the moment I connected the dots as if it happened yesterday. I was watching television and a low-budget swimsuit commercial came on. At its conclusion, a male and female model stood side by side. I felt my eyes drift to the individual on the right—the male model—and it hit me. *The one on the left,* I thought. *I'm supposed to like the one of the left, not the one on the right. I've got it backwards.* Shame and anxiety washed over me.

The sensations that coursed through my body when the church's strikingly attractive welcomer hugged me had been a clue, but I'd missed it at the time. Today, queer people are everywhere you look, in television, music, film, and politics—but this was pre–*Will & Grace* America. I had hardly even heard the word "gay," but when I realized that my eyes gravitated to the swimsuit-wearing man and not the woman, I knew I was *it.*

I resisted, but not for long. Trying to pretend that it wasn't true didn't work; the more I tried not to think about it, the more I fixated on it. It became impossible to deny—I was gay. But even the thought of that word made me bristle.

It seemed too terrible to be true. I had imagined a life in which I would marry a woman and be a proud and dedicated father; that vision crumbled immediately. I spent hours sitting on the crunchy, stubbly green carpet of the local Barnes & Noble, poring over every Christian young adult resource about homosexuality that I could find. Everything I read said the same thing—homosexuality is unnatural, in defiance of God's will, and, well, just gross. There was debate about whether or not it was a choice; most of the resources I found said it was, but I knew it hadn't been for me. The consensus, however, was—choice or not—it was not an acceptable way to live.

And its consequences were grave: should you practice homosexuality, God would afflict you with AIDS, and even if He didn't, He would condemn you to an eternity of suffering in Hell.

I was certain that I hadn't chosen to be gay, but I took these books at their word. It seemed to me that I was afflicted with a spiritual illness of sorts, as if God had decided to test my righteousness or punish me for some awful thing I had done. I lacked exposure to a broader perspective, so I did not understand that Scripture needn't be read as immobile and static. Everything I heard in church and read in books convinced me that there was one correct interpretation of the Bible, and that it spoke clearly on the issue of sexual orientation. Taking the Bible seriously meant taking it literally—and the book of Leviticus literally said that gay people "must be put to death" and that "their blood will be on their own heads."

Early on in my time as a Christian, I asked my discussion-group leader at church which sins were forgivable. He said every sin was forgivable except one: the only unforgivable sin was to hear the word of God and reject Him anyway. I was terrified by this and kept myself under house arrest, guarding my thoughts closely for even an inkling of skepticism or anger or animosity toward God. I could not commit the sin of rejecting Him, or else I would have no chance of making it into heaven. But I also gleaned a sliver of hope from our talk: my same-sex attractions *were* forgivable and, if I could find a way to stop them, I would be redeemed.

I can do this, I told myself daily. *I can earn God's love.*

It turned out my suspicions had been right: there's no such thing as a free lunch. The free pizza at church hadn't been totally free after all—it seemed the free love of Christ and community had strings attached. You always pay a price, but it's good to know the cost before you commit.

As I understood it, this cost was quite literally life and death—after all, Romans 6 instructed that "the wages of sin is death."

I was too young to die, I decided, and so I resolved to find another way to live.

—⁓—

After I had attended youth group every Wednesday night for over a year, my mom decided that the whole family should start going to church. Every Sunday morning after worship, I made a beeline for the church library to see what the latest additions were. I'll admit to enjoying the Veggie Tales' song "Endangered Love (Barbara Manatee)" a little too much, but it was the books that really drew me in. I read Evangelical missives on dating (not that I was doing any), on love, and on how to live in the world—always skipping immediately to the glossary in the back of the book to look for "homosexuality," desperately hoping that even just one book would have something positive to say on the subject.

I never found one.

I started working my way through the Left Behind books, and they were my favorite of all the library had to offer. I tore through each installment with enthusiasm, internalizing its theology and becoming emotionally invested in every character. The Left Behind series imagined the world post-Rapture: a world in chaos, in which the protagonists, realizing the error of their ways, tried to convince the others who had also been left behind to come to Christ and denounce a politician whom they realized was the Antichrist. They were full of characters who had been left behind because they were "casual Christians"—people who had gone to church and believed in God but did not live according to all of God's laws. The devastation they experienced after realizing they had not been good enough felt very real to me and fed into my paranoia about living according to God's laws without exception.

In the third Left Behind book, *Nicolae: The Rise of the Antichrist*, the hero of the series, a scrappy journalist named Buck (whom I had a small crush on until he was portrayed by Kirk Cameron in the *Left Behind* movie) says to an openly lesbian character named Verna: "My Bible doesn't differentiate between homosexuals and heterosexuals . . . It may call practicing homosexuals sinners, but it also calls heterosexual sex outside of marriage sinful."[1]

I was blind-sided by the inclusion of a queer character—especially because, though her depiction was a composite of lesbian stereotypes, Buck's comment to Verna was a sympathetic and perhaps well-intentioned olive branch. But it was clear that his Bible *did* differentiate between homosexuals and heterosexuals, because heterosexual sex within marriage was not sinful while all homosexual sex was. And the character of Verna, though notable, was self-centered and unwilling to listen to the wisdom of her Evangelical Christian friends. She ultimately perished, unsaved. It was an eternity of Hell for her, just as it would be for me.

Her presence and Buck's comment provided a rare glimpse at how the Evangelical movement honestly viewed LGBT people (when not openly despising them): with pity. LGBT people were inferior and less-than; I, on the other hand, wanted to be *more*-than.

My seventh-grade math teacher, a devout Christian, allowed me to sit in her classroom during lunch sometimes so that I could fast and read a Left Behind book (or, more often, my *Teen Study Bible*) while my friends were at lunch. When I fasted, I'd skip breakfast and only allow myself a single piece of sliced bread for lunch; breaking it into pea-sized pieces, I'd consume the bread one tiny bit at a time, holding it in my mouth until it turned to mush, swallowing with great attention, while praying and reading Scripture between each bite.

Most of the time, I'd return to the verses that plagued me: Leviticus 18:22: "Do not have sexual relations with a man as one does with a woman; that is detestable." 1 Corinthians 6:9–10: "Or do you not know that wrongdoers will not inherit the kingdom of God?

Do not be deceived: Neither the sexually immoral nor idolaters nor adulterers nor men who have sex with men nor thieves nor the greedy nor drunkards nor slanderers nor swindlers will inherit the kingdom of God." Leviticus 20:13: "If a man has sexual relations with a man as one does with a woman, both of them have done what is detestable. They are to be put to death; their blood will be on their own heads." Romans 1:26–27: "Because of this, God gave them over to shameful lusts. Even their women exchanged natural sexual relations for unnatural ones. In the same way the men also abandoned natural relations with women and were inflamed with lust for one another. Men committed shameful acts with other men, and received in themselves the due penalty for their error." Genesis 19, or the story of Sodom. Alongside many, my Zondervan *Teen Study Bible* offered commentary that was more explicitly anti-gay than the verses themselves.

"For many people AIDS is a natural consequence of their sinful behavior," I read aloud, sitting beneath a poster highlighting the multiplication table. "Scripture speaks clearly about the homosexual lifestyle. Though many will tell you that homosexuality is a normal alternative lifestyle, God tells you it's a perversion. What people sow they will reap (Galatians 6:7–8)."

I wiped the tears from my face as I hovered over my Bible. All of my friends were in the lunchroom, laughing and eating and having fun, while I sat in an empty classroom, fasting and reading and praying.

"If you stick your hand in a fire and it gets burned, is God punishing you? Or are you simply experiencing the natural consequences of your actions? Statistics show that those who engage in homosexual activities or do drugs with dirty needles or participate in promiscuous sex are at a very high risk for getting AIDS. They've knowingly put their hand in the fire. And they'll probably get burned."[2]

I turned the page, unable to read any more. I was so hungry from fasting—lightheaded and empty.

Without warning, I recalled what my parents had said a year earlier when they sat us down to tell us they were getting divorced.

"We want to make sure you know that this isn't your fault at all," they'd said, and though I didn't yet know anyone else whose parents had gotten a divorce, I already knew that was a cliché.

I had *understood* that their divorce hadn't been my fault, but now I wasn't so sure. Suddenly it seemed possible I had brought all of my own misery upon myself—as if I was responsible for my own suffering, that it was all a consequence for things I had done wrong.

I reopened my *Teen Study Bible*, landing on page 1293. My eyes moved to a sidebar headlined: "The Bible Says: Hell Is for Real!" I read on: "Jesus told his listeners in no uncertain terms that hell is for real. He talked about 'the fire of hell' (Matthew 5:22), and he described someone's 'whole body [going] into hell' (Matthew 5:30). He also told a story about a man who was 'in agony in this fire' (Luke 16:19–31). The Bible mentions three things about hell: It is permanent (Matthew 25:46). It is a punishment for sin and disbelief (2 Thessalonians 1:8). It is separation from God (2 Thessalonians 1:9). The Bible also says that God doesn't want anyone to perish in hell (2 Peter 3:9). God was willing to send his Son to die in order to save everyone who believes from punishment in hell."

I could only conceive of two possible futures for myself: one in which I lived a lonely life in solitude, or one in which I died of AIDS. And both, ultimately, led to the same final future: an eternity in Hell.

The worship album I'd been listening to on my headphones began playing one of my favorite Christian songs, "Light the Fire." I started singing along: "My spirit is willing, but my flesh is so weak."

Momentarily energized by the music, I stood up—and nearly fainted from hunger. I wished I could eat something but that would be a sign of spiritual weakness. If I were to prove my devotion to God and be rewarded by being equipped to overcome this affliction, I'd need to be strong and willing.

But I just felt so weak.

I tried to fight this weakness by being a "strong Christian," believing I could climb the spiritual ladder back into God's good graces if I just worked at it hard enough. Left Behind's Buck had said that "practicing homosexuals" were sinners—so I figured that maybe, with enough effort, I could practice being a good, heterosexual Christian so thoroughly that it would become true in my heart, too.

But my heart was hardening, steeling itself with calluses against the damage I was inflicting on myself. I couldn't pray the gay away, no matter how hard I tried. I loved going to church; I was very active in the community and seen as a true and dutiful lover of God. However, just beneath the surface my pot was about to boil over.

My mom, usually so aware when something was amiss, had too many boiling pots of her own to notice mine. Because she was working multiple jobs while studying to become an insurance agent she couldn't be around as much as she used to. I moved rooms to share with one of my younger brothers so that we could host a college student who lived with us rent free in exchange for watching my siblings and me a few nights a week. We did this for a number of years, with a different student each year. There were two colleges nearby, and both were highly religious schools with strict policies on drinking, recreational activities, and even the number of feet required on the floor when people of opposite genders were in a dorm room together (three).

The young women who lived with us were exceptionally kind, though quite different from one another. The first, Jennifer, introduced me to Garbage's self-titled debut album; though it wasn't Christian music, I loved it—and Jennifer covered for me when I bought their Parental Advisory–labeled *Version 2.0*. She helped me dye my hair for the first time and inspired me to get my eyebrow pierced (I didn't keep it long, fortunately). Jennifer was a Christian but told me that she had liberal views on certain things and that I shouldn't worry so much about reading the Bible so literally. It was a nice thought, but caught up in my own zealous, inflexible interpretation, I didn't absorb it.

The next boarder celebrated my zeal for Scripture, creating flash cards for me when I told her I wanted to work on memorizing verses. Short-haired and joyous, Amy's eyes lit up as we discussed the Book of Romans while walking the dog. I loved our conversations about God and the Bible, and was always asking her to help me learn more about Jesus's life.

The third, a sweet woman and truly gifted chef responsible for perhaps the best fried rice I've had to this day, was the most conservatively Christian of all. I avoided talking politics with her because, as a born-and-raised Democrat, I was worried she might think I wasn't a good Christian.

I was a different person with each of these houseguests, but my circumspection wasn't confined to my home; I avoided talking about a lot of things with a lot of people. I was terrified that someone would discover the truth about my sexual orientation, so I built a wall between myself and the world around me. Everything I said and did became performance—I was an actor inhabiting my own life, trying to put forth the image of a good, devoted Christian. I played dcTalk's "Jesus Freak" on my Discman and hummed along loudly, wallpapered my textbooks in Bible-based bumper stickers, relished my free subscription to *Contemporary Christian Music* magazine, and wore pins that said "Jesus: King of Kings" in the Reese's Peanut Butter Cups font. I ardently avoided anything that didn't align with this image—and I especially avoided anything associated with gay stereotypes.

One day I overheard someone at school say that my best friend, Jake, was a fag. Starting that day, I began to pull away from Jake. Coming home that afternoon, I told my mom that everyone at school thought Jake was gay because he liked Britney Spears (but not in *that* way) and Sailor Moon, and that I was worried he might be.

"Well, he might be," she said, glancing up from her book with a slight shrug.

That was it. She didn't really say anything more than that. I suspect she didn't think there was more at work in my bringing it up. But in my desperate fear and crippling insecurity, I heard her say something entirely different: *Well, Jake might be gay—but you'd better not be, or else I won't love you anymore.*

My closeted, queer, adolescent, Christian mind was not a rational one. It was ruled by fear. Fear of who I was, fear that I could not change, and fear of anyone discovering my struggle.

As the years went by, my life became an increasingly uninhabitable mess. Normally a dedicated and enthusiastic student, I grew uninterested in school. Jake wasn't the only friend I avoided—I began to withdraw from most of my relationships. I spent many evenings in my bedroom with a Bible, two highlighters, a pen, and a notebook. In yellow, I highlighted verses in the Bible that gave me hope that I might be rid of my same-sex attractions. I took respite in passages like 2 Corinthians 5:17, which said, "Therefore, if anyone is in Christ, the new creation has come: The old has gone, the new is here." In green, I highlighted verses that made me feel discouraged, like verses condemning homosexuality. I also highlighted Romans 12:2 in green—"Do not conform to the pattern of this world, but be transformed by the renewing of your mind. Then you will be able to test and approve what God's will is—His good, pleasing and perfect will." I felt depressed that I could not live up to God's perfect will but was, instead, trapped by my "worldly" inclinations. I scrawled in my notebook, trying to come up with ways to change my orientation, writing dismayed letters to no one. The irony, of course, was that I had first come to Christianity looking for community. It had never been about pizza or even popularity, really—I was just looking for a place to belong, and a way to make sense of injustice. But instead I retreated within myself, inhabiting a false story and hoping no one would see behind the curtain.

And so I found myself avoiding friends and loved ones—it was easier to maintain the illusion that I was a happy, heterosexual Christian if people didn't see me.

"You coming to youth group tonight?" My friend's voice sounded distorted coming through the phone's speaker.

"Maybe," I said in a kind of drawl. "I might just stay home tonight and do my own Bible study."

"But you've done that the last few weeks," she said, groaning. I could picture her on the other end—decked out in her favorite Jesus fish t-shirt, four "WWJD?" bracelets on each wrist, and a Bible by her side—running her hands through her thin auburn hair, closing her eyes tight, and pinching her forehead. She sounded anxious.

"Are you okay, Tiffer? I feel like I never see you anymore. We all miss you at church!"

"I'm great!" I replied, too quickly. "Of course, I'm just fine!" I scrambled to reassure her, practically yelling.

"Well, we're going to be talking about what makes a Christly man this week," she said, "so I just thought you'd be interested."

I was, of course, but it was too late for me. I knew what being a Christly man meant, and I wasn't it. Instead of answering, I reached under my bed and pulled out a collection of childhood artifacts my mom had assembled for me, retrieving a worksheet I'd filled out in second grade. *When I grow up*, it said in a passable attempt at cursive, *I want to be: A dad. Because: I want a family.*

Stupid, naïve kid, I thought, shuddering. *You'll never have that.* I put the worksheet away and pulled out my study Bible, turning once more to Leviticus.

"I think I just need some one-on-one time with God tonight, you know?"

"I know," she said. But she didn't; no one knew. I had become an adept liar—or, at least, a consistent one. My life had become a performance, a play I was writing as I went along, calculated to invoke a particular perception: that I was happy, normal, straight, and Christian.

After a minute of silence, a voice emerged from the phone.

"You still there?"

"Yes," I said, voice cracking. "I'm still here." Another lie.

Growing more and more frustrated that I was perpetually posing and not seeing any hope of change, I became wholeheartedly despondent. I kept praying and fasting, waiting to wake up straight, but I was at the end of my rope. I did everything the books I read told me to, but my same-sex attractions were not changing. I became convinced that this was a yoke I'd carry my whole life, and I was tired of suffering.

In a moment of deep despair, I grabbed a knife and toyed with ending my life. I was spending the night at my father's apartment; my siblings were asleep and my father was out at a bar. I took the knife into the bathroom, turned on the fan, and bolted the door shut. I walked to the shower, slid the glass door open, and sat down inside, sliding the door shut behind me. This was the shower in which I furtively masturbated, filled with shame and self-loathing, thinking of men and hoping God was distracted at the moment. I looked through the glass; the room just beyond was a blur, obscured by soap scum. The house was silent, except for the drip of the faucet and the sound of air rapidly entering and exiting my nostrils. I wiped the snot running down my lip with the rolled-up right sleeve of the "Acquire the Fire" sweatshirt I was wearing.

Holding the weighty metal blade in my right hand, I ran the dull side along my left wrist, like I was taking it for a test drive. The metal, like the shower floor, was cold. I flipped the knife over so that the sharp side was facing down, across my wrist, and sliced it through the air above my flesh, again trying the motion on for size. I had seen this in a few movies, though it usually seemed a bit more romantic—an eloquent note left by the sink, a bathtub full of soapy water to hide one's nakedness, two tidily slit wrists blossoming with blood, an expression of serenity on the deceased's face.

This hardly felt so noble: me, crouched in the shower in the middle of the night, holding a rusted knife used for chopping carrots, mopping up the tears and snot trickling down my face with my sleeve, and listening carefully for any sound suggesting my dad had arrived home or that someone had woken up to use the bathroom, guided only by adrenaline and impulse and anguish. I set the knife on the floor beside me and realized I had no idea what I was doing. *How does this even work?* I asked, almost aloud, not wanting to know the answer.

I couldn't will myself to go through with it. I was too afraid—of the selfishness of this act and how my family would react to it; of the physical pain involved; of failing at this, too; but most of all of the fate I was sure would greet me after death. I already had a strike against me for lusting after men, but suicide would seal the deal. And I didn't really want to die; that night, slouched in the shower, holding a blade I'd hoped would end my suffering, all I wanted was to bury the knife in the backyard where I would never have to see it again, to smile as much as I used to, to be held and loved by someone who could fix it all for me.

I couldn't work up the nerve to end my own life, yet I wasn't really living. I stumbled through life like a zombie, totally disconnected from what was going on around me, fixated on changing something I could not, seeking solace in the Bible, in prayer, in worshipping a God I was sure was disgusted by me. I could find no relief. Surrounding myself with people who saw me as the perfect Christian, I felt trapped within my own lie of a life—one I could not bring myself to end, but one I could not go on living.

—◦◦◦—

I finally came out of the closet because my actual closet was messy.

My mom was something of a stickler when it came to how we kept our rooms. Anytime she demanded that I clean my room because it was getting too messy, I thought I could outsmart her by shoving my clutter to the back corners of the floor beneath my bed and in my closet. She always knew to look there, though, so I don't know why I imagined it was so clever every time. I always regretted my corner-cutting whenever I'd walk into my room and find a garbage bag full of my belongings in the center of the floor with a note threatening to throw them out if I didn't put them in their proper places before she returned home.

On one such cleaning spree in April, right before my fourteenth birthday, she found the notebook in which I'd been detailing my agony and read some of its contents. Many moms do this, yes, but she had good reason: she'd watched her loud, self-confident, and joyous son become a shell of a person over the short span of just a few years.

So the next day, after a session of Red Cross lifeguard training, I got into our car with her, ready to brag about how I had pulled a classmate twice my size out of the water in a drill. Instead, she said: "We need to talk." Those words could only mean one thing—I was in big trouble.

My heart leapt into the back of my throat and I swallowed hard to hold it at bay. I knew this day would come but I never thought it would be so soon. I was sure that it was the moment I'd feared more than anything. I started to mentally catalogue everything I had loved about my family and prepared to say goodbye to it all. *This is it*, I thought to myself, *you're on your own now. Time to grow up and take care of yourself.* But I wasn't ready to say goodbye to my childhood. How could I take care of myself when I didn't even love myself? Before she even said another word, I began to sob.

It was the ultimate cosmic injustice that I would lose everything and everyone that I loved—my family, my church community, my friends—all over something I could not control. *How could God give me a family only to take it away from me?*

I took a deep breath and steeled myself for what I knew was coming. In my mind, I heard the words my mom had never actually said echoing in my head: *Well, Jake might be gay—but you'd better not be, or else I won't love you anymore.*

After a long pause, she finally said, "I found your journal."

My mouth went dry. My forehead, damp with the combination of chlorinated water and perspiration, flushed with a miserable warmth. I felt every single hair on my arm—there weren't many—stand on end, vibrating and quivering with an unwanted awareness of what was happening. A police siren blared on the highway behind the parking lot where we sat in the car, sounding the alarm that somewhere nearby there was an emergency.

I didn't want her to reject me, but I felt like I'd earned it. I didn't deserve love—not from God, not from my mom, not from anyone. I was worse than dirt; even earth had a purpose in God's creation. I was an aberration, an unlovable abomination.

I buried my face in my thighs, hugging my legs tight in an attempt to curl up into a ball in the front seat of the car. Breathing in the chlorine smell of my swimsuit, I wanted to disappear into the cold wet cave of my lap. I couldn't bear the harsh light of the truth.

I didn't want to see my mother's face twisted by shame and disgust. I wanted more than anything to make her proud. She had given up everything for me, and how had I returned the favor? The sinner son; the kind no parent wants.

I sobbed and shook, the whole world quaking with me. After years of feeling so utterly alone, it suddenly felt like it had been a gift to carry the burden of my secret on my own. The sheer loneliness of those years didn't compare to the immense weight of shame that came from knowing that the most important person in my life now knew my deep, dark, detestable secret. I couldn't have torn my face from my lap even if I'd wanted to; I knew that, as soon as I did, all of this would be real. For a moment more I was safe in the dark, me and my secrets, so closely guarded, so tightly bound.

I felt the light touch of my mother's hand on my back.

"I love you, and nothing will ever change that," she said, and I couldn't stop shaking.

What had started as an attempt by my mother to clean out my bedroom closet became an airing of the dirty laundry I'd stuffed back into the dusty back corners of my life, the mess I'd hidden to try to show the world a clean exterior. My mom, as she always did, had seen right through the thicket of my tricks; she knew I had not actually been cleaning up after myself, that I had instead kept the contents of my life tucked away, disconnected from all who loved me. To my mom, honesty mattered. My father had been a secret smoker for a good part of their marriage, but upon discovering this, she was less disturbed by the cigarettes than she was by my father's need to do it in secret and lie when asked about it.

There was no way to lie my way out of this. She had read my crisis, in my own words, in my messy, self-loathing script. There was no explaining this away.

We didn't say much more that night; I was exhausted from crying and sick to my stomach. When I was finally able to pull my face out of the shadows, she drove me home. I got out of the car and stumbled downstairs to my room, locking the door behind me. It was obvious that my mom had discovered my notebook in the middle of cleaning; there was a garbage bag in the middle of the room only partially filled, sitting open like a gaping mouth, and most of my mess remained in the back corner of my closet. I took the Bible from my nightstand and threw it atop the pile of papers on my closet floor. Shutting the closet door, I turned off my bedroom light and pulled the bedcovers over my head, hugging my pillow like I had wanted to hug my mom.

The next morning, I slept in. My mom didn't come down to wake me up for school as she so often had to, my body refusing to rise at the sound of my alarm most mornings. Eventually I woke up and, after lying in bed for an hour staring at the spackled ceiling, I got out and went upstairs.

My mom was sitting at the kitchen table with a glass of water, working on some insurance paperwork. She looked up at me and said: "I scheduled a meeting with a minister. Let's go."

I followed her to the car, opened the passenger door, and climbed in. Still in my pajamas, I sat in the car silently, running through the possible outcomes of this meeting. *Who was this minister? Was he going to try to cure me of my disorder? Was he going to fix me?* After what my mom had said the night before, it didn't seem likely that she'd be sending me off to reparative-therapy camp, but I couldn't fathom the possibility that a minister could be anything but antigay. I looked out the right side of the car and saw a swarm of black terns rise from the marsh I had often explored with my siblings. Out the left window, we passed the community center parking lot where just last night my mom had broken open the lock on my secret life. In less than twenty-four hours, everything had changed. I didn't feel like a child anymore, yet I wasn't an adult. I was in between worlds, lost.

We pulled into the parking lot of Incarnation Lutheran Church, right next door to the middle school I'd graduated from the year before, and stopped the car in an empty spot. My mom came around to my side of the car, opened the door, and motioned for me to exit. She gave me a hug, took my hand, and led me to the front door of the church. I walked alongside her in a daze, blinded by the bright spring sun shining down on us.

I stopped at the entrance and looked up at the giant crucifix on the building's front face. Two thousand and two or so years ago, Jesus had died on a cross very much like it; I would turn fourteen in a week, and, for the first time since my conversion, I cringed at the sight of this ancient symbol.

"We're here to see Pastor Luther Dale," my mom said. I stared at the maroon rug at my feet, unable to look at the secretary, convinced she knew why I was there. My face flushed with embarrassment at the thought of anyone else knowing my secret.

"Right this way," I heard her say. Then, the shuffle of feet and my mom's hand grabbing mine to lead me down the hall to an office filled with books and framed Bible verses.

Pastor Dale had gray, curly hair and wore a big smile. He sat in a desk chair and motioned for my mother and me to sit on a floral-patterned couch.

"Your mother called me yesterday and let me know you've been struggling with something," he said, cautiously.

I turned bright red and looked down at my feet.

"Would you like me to leave you two alone?" my mom asked me. After nearly a minute, I nodded. I didn't know what to think. She put her arm around my shoulder, squeezed me tight, and walked out of the room. She stopped at the door, turned around, and said she'd be out in the office reception if I needed her.

I sat on the couch with my arms crossed tightly across my chest. After another minute of my silence, he raised the issue again.

"You know, I know this is a tough issue. One of my closest friends struggled with it for a long time."

I looked up and he nodded.

"My best friend and roommate in college was gay," Pastor Dale said, exhaling and crossing one of his legs over the other. "He had always been a little quiet, and didn't ever really share much about his personal life. Then one night, near the end of college, he came out to me. He said he had struggled with it all of his life, and that he finally couldn't keep it in any longer and needed to tell someone.

"I know that I can't even begin to imagine how difficult this is for you," he said, looking pained. "But I want you to know that there are people who care about you a whole lot, like your mom, and who love you just the way that God made you. They don't want you to change, and neither does God."

He grabbed my *Teen Study Bible* out of my hands; I stared at the floor.

"'Alternative lifestyle' usually refers to making a sexual choice," he said, reading aloud from the book. "The impression is that any choice is all right. It's just a matter of preference." He sighed loudly.

"When it comes to sex, don't kid yourself about some of those choices being morally all right: It's wrong to have sex with any close relative. It's wrong to have sex with animals. It's wrong to have homosexual sex." He sighed again, longer and louder.

"This isn't the only Bible passage that says homosexual sex is a sin. Read also Romans 1:26–27. If someone tells you homosexuality is an alternative lifestyle—meaning that it's OK—don't let those words fool you. It's an alternative all right. A sinful one."[3]

After a final sigh, he delicately lifted a red pen from his desk and drew strong, deliberate red lines over the entire page, creating a giant X.

"This is dehumanizing garbage," he said. "Being gay isn't like incest or bestiality. Jesus would be flipping tables in the authors' offices over this."

I looked up from the floor and, for the first time in far too long, genuinely smiled.

I couldn't really take in what I was hearing. Here was a Man of God, with the collar to prove it, saying that God had *made* me this way.

Here, finally, was someone in a position of religious authority telling me that there was nothing unnatural about my sexual orientation. But after a moment, instead of feeling relieved, I felt angry.

If God had made me this way, why did He allow me to suffer so much? Why did He let people claiming to speak on His behalf convince me that I was immoral and unworthy of His love? Why did His Holy Book call me an abomination? Why had He not intervened when I was so desperate for any kind of a sign telling me that I wasn't the scum of the earth?

After we were finished, Pastor Dale offered to meet again anytime but also referred me to a friend of his, a Lutheran counselor, whom I started to see on a monthly basis. He and I talked about sexual orientation, and he helped me to understand that the overwhelming agreement among licensed psychologists is that homosexuality is natural. But I left God out of our counseling sessions, responding when asked that I didn't want to talk about Him.

The burden of believing I was a monster and the struggle of dealing with that conflict in secret was over. I felt liberated, as if the demons had been cast out of me. After years of speaking with other LGBTQ people, I know that my situation was the exception to the rule. So many people I've met have been rejected by their families and their churches; many ultimately even reject themselves. I believe in many ways that my mom and Pastor Dale saved my life, and I remain grateful that my mom chose love over fear.

—◊—

These meetings began at the end of my freshman year of high school, a milestone of adolescence. Due to construction on my school, my freshman year had started several weeks late. Because of this, on September 11, 2001, I woke up early, prayed, and sat down on the couch to watch the morning news, not needing to go to school. I turned on the television and was greeted by live footage of the World Trade Center in New York City, a gaping, smoking wound in the side of one of the buildings. The newscasters were calling it a terrible accident, but a feeling in the pit of my empty stomach told me something unimaginably horrifying was happening. Then, right before my eyes, a second plane flew into the World Trade Center.

After being glued to my television for several hours, I walked into my backyard and lay down in the grass. Staring into the sky, afraid to see an airplane pass between the strands of cloud overhead, I asked God to protect all Americans, but especially the people in New York City, Washington, D.C., and Pennsylvania. For the first time in years, my mind had shifted away from worrying about my sexuality, and my prayer was a petition for the well-being of others.

That school year started with a life-altering national trauma—a dark cloud hanging over the head of every American that will continue to shape our nation's discourse for years to come. So my mom's confrontation with me at the end of my first year of high school felt like an appropriate capstone to a year that signified the beginning of my transition from childhood into adulthood. But though I turned to God on September 11, 2001, I wanted nothing to do with Him by the end of that academic year.

I still believed in God, but after learning that there were multiple interpretations of the passages in the Bible that purportedly address homosexuality, I believed His willingness to let me go on suffering so long meant that He was either malevolent and vicious, or detached and unconcerned with my well-being. I didn't want to go to church; He was a bully, and going to His house was the last thing I wanted.

I had stepped out of the closet and out of the Church, and I had no desire to ever set foot in either one again.

4

Losing and Finding My Religion

If you can achieve puberty, you can achieve a past.

—DOLLY PARTON

With my secret struggle over my sexual orientation and Christian beliefs brought to light and addressed, I felt completely disillusioned with the Church. In many ways I considered God, as the Church's founder, the root of the problem. I stopped attending services and stopped praying, adopting apathy in place of the time I had spent trying to climb the religious ladder out of sin and into God's good grace. I still believed in God, but I was tired of thinking about Him.

My sister, however, was experiencing something of a personal spiritual revival. She had been invited to attend a weekend retreat run by an organization called Minnesota Metro Lutheran Teens Encounter Christ and had fallen in love with it. After watching me morph from social butterfly to social husk, my mom decided it'd be a good opportunity for me to get together with other people. I protested, but I knew from the beginning that she'd win out.

I arrived at the church to find an enthusiastic group of high schoolers with brightly colored shirts and Colgate smiles. As usual, I was wearing pajama pants—it was my sheepish way of rebelling against what I thought was expected of me. I peered through the car window as the teens shouted and waved to me, wondering if I could make a last-minute bargain with my mom to keep driving past the church in exchange for a commitment to keep my room clean forever.

After parking the car, my mom told me to buck up and go inside. I was overwhelmed. As a child, I'd been gregarious and self-confident—but after years of holing myself up in my room with a Bible, of isolating myself from the rest of the world both physically and emotionally, I'd forgotten how to be sociable.

Brushing past the welcoming committee with a closed-mouth smile, I brought my bags to my room, spread out my sleeping bag, and put on my headphones. After sitting there for about fifteen minutes, a guy not too much older than me walked over and motioned for me to remove my headphones.

"Hey," he said, casually easing himself on to the floor next to me. "I'm Karl."

"Hey, Karl," I said. "I'm Tiffer."

"That's an unusual name," he said.

"Yeah," I replied. "My sister couldn't say 'Christopher' when we were kids, and everyone thought it was cute, so it stuck."

"It *is* cute," he said, laughing.

I tried not to blush, worried that my face would soon match his striking red hair. I decided he was cuter than any nickname.

"Wait—are you Christopher Stedman?" he asked.

"Yeah, that's me," I said. "Why?"

"Oh, I'm your YTL, Youth Table Leader," he said. "We're going to be hanging out all weekend."

With that, I actually did blush. *Great*, I thought. *I'm going to be even more awkward now. I have to act normal, though, because if he finds out I'm gay, he'll freak out.*

"Come on—let's go meet Randy, our Adult Table Leader."

We made our way to a large room where the majority of retreat activities would take place, passing an immense number of chipper greetings and hand waves. Karl approached a short man with a reddish face; he seemed happier than anyone else there. He laughed when Karl elbowed him, his guffaws bursting out with the volume and force of a lion's roar. I steeled myself for a long and wearying weekend.

As the retreat kicked off, I was incredibly skeptical of the gusto Randy, Karl, and nearly everyone else seemed to exhibit, the fervor they poured into the songs and games. I was also experiencing flashbacks to my initial conversion several years prior. But, as the weekend went on, I began to warm to the program. After just one day, I begrudgingly admitted to myself that these were among the most genuinely kind and open-hearted individuals I had ever met, and when I finally let down my cynical guard, the activities actually *were* a lot of fun.

For a moment, however, it seemed that all of that would be washed away as—following a talk on the second day—a debate about homosexuality flared up like a Great Plains wildfire. As words flew back and forth across the room, I sat there staring off into space, trying to stop the blood from rushing to my face.

I knew this would happen, I thought to myself. *I knew things were going too well. I told my mom that I wouldn't be welcomed here. Almost all Christians are homophobic.*

An adult stepped in to divert the conversation. Things settled down, and we were split up into our small groups, with Karl and Randy shepherding my group into a tight circle.

"Hey guys, I'm really sorry that happened," Karl said, and I could swear he was looking directly at me.

We were all quiet.

"I just want you folks to know that there's a lot of disagreement about this issue," Randy said, his face dominated by a monumental grin. "And, well, you know, there are a lot of competing claims within the tradition. But I feel like it's important that I let you know that I'm gay."

Everything stopped: my breath, my heart, and all of the action around me. My attention focused only on his words and blocked out everything else like horse blinders—other kids running by, whooping and hollering, Christian hip-hop blaring from down the hall—and I heard only those words. *I'm. Gay.*

I could've wept. It was as if our meeting was a portent; like God Himself had sent me to this retreat and put me at this table so that I could meet another gay Christian.

After our group disbanded—there was rumor of a dance party—I asked Randy if we could talk in private. We spent hours sitting outside the church watching cars drive by, tracking the sun as it inched its way closer and closer to the horizon until it was finally subsumed and the night sky reigned. As I confided in him, I felt the hole in my heart slowly filling back up. It was one thing to hear that it was okay to be gay from a straight Christian minister, but meeting someone who could relate experientially to the struggles I had faced was something else altogether. I recalled 1 Corinthians 13:12: "For now we see only a reflection as in a mirror; then we shall see face to face. Now I know in part; then I shall know fully, even as I am fully known."

I felt known; I felt human again.

—∿—

My mom's prediction had been realized: I left Teens Encounter Christ feeling as if I had a new group of lifelong best friends. I quickly decided to return to volunteer at a TEC retreat. I had a wonderful time that weekend but didn't feel ready to tell anyone that I was gay. But as the weekend went on and I witnessed so many people opening up about their struggles, I felt the need to be honest.

So I applied to work at another retreat; this time, I told the organizers that I'd like to give the "God is Love" talk. I was placed on the Wheat Team—the group of people who staffed the prayer room—and was approved to give the talk.

I was warned that I'd be expected to give a "practice talk"—a dry run of the talk I'd do on the weekend—at the first pre-TEC meeting, which was a gathering of all of the volunteers. I prepared for weeks, writing and rewriting my talk. I emptied all of the anguish I had known, the rejection I had felt, all of my self-loathing, and transformed it into hope and optimism, into a call for love and acceptance. I began and ended with 1 John 4:8: "Whoever does not love does not know God, because God is love."

I walked into the meeting and looked around. There were some folks I knew from my first TEC—Karl among them—and from the one I had volunteered at, but most were strangers. My stomach tightened. I wanted to turn around and walk out, but I told myself that I couldn't give up. *If not for myself, I need to do this for others*, I thought. *What if there is someone in this group who is struggling with her or his sexuality? I could give that person the same comfort Randy gave me. Or maybe someone will hear my talk and give another person comfort down the road.*

After some mingling, it was time for me to give my talk. I walked to the front of the room and sat down in a chair facing the group. Before the talk started, I played a Christian song, as was customary for all TEC talks. As Audio Adrenaline's "Pierced" swelled, my eyes welled up, and I began to sob uncontrollably.

I was terrified. After years of hiding, honesty was hard—and the kind of complete, soul-baring candor I wanted to convey seemed impossible. My sister walked to the front of the room and took a seat beside me, taking my hand.

Standing before a crowd of faces both familiar and foreign, I turned inward to muster my deepest courage.

"For a long time, I didn't think I deserved God's love," I said, choking on my words. "Because I'm gay."

I wasn't even out to my entire family or most of my friends, and here I was, sixteen years old, saying those words before a group of fifty acquaintances and strangers. I felt a rush and wondered if this was what my fellow Christians meant when they talked about letting the Holy Spirit lead you into testimony.

It was too late to turn back. And so I pressed on, detailing the weight of self-hatred I had felt and, in closing, sharing my optimism about the liberating potential of love:

> During that first TEC weekend, my table leader shared a Bible verse with me. 1 John 4:7–12 says: "Dear friends, let us love one another, for love comes from God. Everyone who loves has been born of God and knows God. Whoever does not love does not know God, because God is love. This is how God showed his love among us: He sent his one and only Son into the world that we might live through him. This is love: not that we loved God, but that he loved us and sent his Son as an atoning sacrifice for our sins. Dear friends, since God so loved us, we also ought to love one another. No one has ever seen God; but if we love one another, God lives in us and his love is made complete in us." If God is love, and His love is fulfilled when we love one another, then it is impossible for Him to hate any of His creations or for us to hate one another. He loves each and every one of us because He is love, and we are supposed to follow His lead.
>
> After years of hating myself for who I am, and hating others because I felt different, I'm finally able to wrap my mind around this concept. I left my first TEC retreat with many new friends, but more importantly, knowing that God loves everyone—even me. And I am supposed to do the same to others.

After I had finished, I received a hug from nearly everyone in the room. There were, of course, some ruffled feathers—I later heard that a few of the adult volunteers who had been very kind to my face actually threatened to quit TEC—but for the most part, the community boldly and lovingly supported me. After my talk, a pastor approached my mom and said: "Before meeting Tiffer, I strongly believed gay people didn't belong in the church. But after getting to know him and hearing him talk about his experiences, I've changed my mind. Thank you for raising him to be the person he is."

In addition to my involvement in TEC, I started attending a support group for queer Christian youth in Minneapolis called The Naming Project. The Naming Project was housed at Bethany Lutheran Church, a "Reconciling Congregation" (meaning one that supports the total inclusion of queer folks in church life) with a gay minister. Both the church and the support group became my safe havens and their facilitators became my closest mentors. They modeled what it could look like to live a fulfilled and happy life as a queer person. I attended nearly every Sunday for the remainder of high school, and when they decided to host a summer camp for LGBTQ teens, I signed up immediately. A camera crew documented the week, which resulted in the award-winning documentary film *Camp Out*.

I became an energetic queer Christian activist. I went on to serve as a codirector for a TEC retreat, was elected to TEC council, and spoke at conferences on LGBT and Christian issues. This activism eventually landed me on the cover of Minneapolis-St. Paul's LGBTQ magazine. Because of this my mom was called in for a meeting with our pastor, who suggested I might be more comfortable at another church. This didn't bother me as much as it did my mom; I had already found a church of my own that felt like home.

In many ways, I began to feel like an adult. Because my high school had been a terrifying place to be a queer kid, I got out as soon as I could, spending the last two years doing the majority of my coursework at a local community college through a state program. This gave me a lot of freedom and flexibility. I spent afternoons working at a Scandinavian bakery and café, took night classes, and dedicated my weekends to volunteering at TEC and interning for a drop-in center for LGBTQ youth run by the St. Paul Public School District.

I had my own car, my own money, and friends who were older than eighteen and would buy me clove cigarettes. But I also felt like a child—especially when it came to dating. Early in my junior year of high school, I went on a date to see *Garden State* with a guy named Jake. He had offered to pick me up from home, so there was no way around telling my mother. The afternoon of our date, I told her whom I was meeting up with. She raised an eyebrow and took a long breath. Moments later, Jake texted me to let me know he was waiting in the driveway. I hugged my mom goodbye and bolted out the front door, hoping she wouldn't feel compelled to follow me outside. As I slid into the passenger seat—or stumbled clumsily, rather, as I've never been anything close to suave—I looked past my date to the living room and spotted my mom peering through the curtains. A few minutes later, my phone rang. I answered and heard my mother's voice: "I'd say the same thing to your heterosexual sister, but you are *not* allowed to go back to his apartment." I laughed, but I also didn't dare betray her rule.

It was funny, but it also reflected the reality that despite all the amazing things that she'd done for me, my mom was uncertain about how to raise a gay son. It wasn't her fault—she just didn't feel entirely equipped to do so. Parenting a gay teenager wasn't widely discussed or modeled; she had no resources.

But without that guidance, I didn't know how to be gay, either. Sitting in a darkened theater and watching *Garden State,* I moved my elbow away when Jake's arm brushed mine. Six months later, when I finally got my first kiss from a guy named Charlie, I panicked and didn't call him back after he reached into my pants the second time we made out behind a queer teen drop-in center.

But in my senior year of high school, I met someone different. Jon showed up at a TNP meeting one day, and everyone else in the room disappeared. We locked eyes and I rarely looked elsewhere for the rest of the meeting. I said little that afternoon until, as we were preparing to leave, I asked him if he might want to hang out sometime. We traded information, and that night we talked for hours. We did the same the next day and, four long days later, we had our first date. That date was followed by another a week later, and then another, and then many more.

By all accounts, I was finally living the life I'd spent years imagining I'd never have—one of honesty, one in which I lived fearlessly into the breadth of who I was. And after years of watching my straight friends explore what it meant to relate to others romantically, I was able to explore that for myself.

But like many other times I thought I had finally gotten a grip on things, my newfound sense of balance would soon slip between my fingers.

—᚛᚛—

The morning after my eighteenth birthday party, my first boyfriend—the one I had fallen for immediately; who told me that God brought us together and made me believe it; whom I cared about so deeply that four weeks into our relationship I dug out the certificate I had cosigned with God agreeing not to have sex before marriage from the bottom of my underwear drawer, scattering green and orange boxers across my camel carpet, and triumphantly tore it in two; the one for whom I only applied to in-state colleges; the one I thought I'd marry—broke up with me in a text message.

I blinked, trying to make it not true, and thought back to the end of our second date—to the first time we kissed. After a night of nervous conversation buffered by watching a play that had brought the relief of silence, we stood before our cars, positioned side-by-side in an open-air parking garage. We shuffled our feet and looked down at the yellow line beneath us (which I imagined as an impassible barrier), glancing up just long enough to lock eyes before flicking them back down, hearts pounding, palms clammy, dragging out our conversation until we both fell silent. He walked to the driver's door of the car he had borrowed from a friend and got in, then pressed a button to unlock the passenger door and motioned for me to join him inside. The click of the lock snapping open reverberated between the parking garage's concrete pillars. I looked at my car, then back at him, and climbed in. I settled in and fumbled with the seatbelt before realizing I wasn't going to need it. I shivered from the cold and my nerves. The floor mat beneath my feet was gravelly and cracked, and I envisioned one of the splits opening up like the Red Sea; if I moved now, I'd finally find freedom, but if I stayed immobile much longer I might be swallowed whole, cast to the bottom of a red sea of hesitation. I sat motionless, eyes cast down, my breathing short, sharp, and excited.

Jon interrupted the silence with words spilling and spitting and stumbling over one another like waves of upset dominoes.

"Okay, Chris! We have to kiss! I will not let you out of this car unless we've kissed!"

"I know!" I said. "But I'm scared!"

Jon grinned. "Me too," he said. "I keep asking myself, 'what if I'm a bad kisser?'"

"I doubt that very much," I said, smirking in a weak attempt to project confidence. Then, a thought: *What if he is a bad kisser?* Worse still: *What if I am?*

"Only one way to find out," he said, his eyes like summer sparklers. "It has to happen tonight. It can't wait any longer."

"You're right," I replied, my thumbs pressed against one another in a blush of pink and white. "I don't want to wait any longer either."

"But you have to kiss me because I've never been kissed before," he said.

"I can do that," I said, smiling hard and swallowing harder.

"Okay, we can't do this because it has to be spontaneous and new and whatever, so let's start a different conversation," Jon said.

I laughed, but it was half-hearted. I was scared. The possibility that this kiss could go poorly—that it could undo our budding romance—was paralyzing.

But instead of vocalizing any of that, I said, "So that play was pretty cool tonight, eh? I really liked the songs."

"Yeah, they were pretty good," he said, leaning in a bit, rocking back and forth ever so slightly, like a racer on the starting blocks. His eyes said: *Go, Chris! Now, Chris! Hurry up!*

I was still scared, frozen like the ice crystals splayed across the windshield, so I continued: "Yeah, and the story was great." A plane flew overhead, full of people listening to Nickelback on their Discmans and flipping the pages of some Dan Brown novel, clueless to the milestone moment going on below their buckled waists.

"Uh huh," he said, while his eyes pleaded with me to move.

"And your friend, the one in the show—he was great! A really good actor, yeah," I said, stammering.

"Yep," Jon said, staring me in the mouth, waiting for me to lean forward with my eyes closed and end this charade.

"And the props . . ." I started.

"Kiss me kiss me kiss me!" Jon exclaimed, unable to wait any longer. And I did. In that moment, the world split open. It was like the first time I successfully rode my bike without feeling like I would topple over in an instant; like the first time I read a book or listened to a song and really *felt* it; like the first time a word emerged amongst the gibberish of my infant mouth. All of those years I had been told that homosexuality was immoral and unnatural washed away with the initial mash of our lips. It wasn't my first kiss, but it was the first that meant anything, and with it I knew that this was, for me, the most natural thing in the world. We kept kissing—dizzy and messy, tumbling over our laughter, arms in the wrong places, foreheads bumping, reuniting every time we tried to pull apart—until I was very late for my curfew.

And now, I would never kiss him again. Just like that—a set of words on a screen about his parents' discovery, about sickness and forbidden sin—and it was done.

I thought back to the nights we walked down dusk-lit streets and extended our good-byes as long as possible so that time became something that only applied to other people, as if we had uncovered the secret to evading the restraints that kept others at the mercy of hours and minutes and seconds; to the times we spoke on the phone, voices cracking over a crackling wireless connection, longing to be together, happy just to hear one another sigh as we compared ourselves to the biblical David and Jonathan—to how he had cured me of the loneliness that had plagued me from the moment I knew I was queer.

I thought back to the first few months of our relationship and how I would listen to Christian rock band Relient K's "I Am Understood?" earnestly, in disbelief that, for the first time in my life, there was someone who experientially understood what it was like to grow up gay and religious, and who loved me *because* of the person I was, not in spite of it. I thought back to every time he had made me feel like a normal teenager with a normal boyfriend. To how lucky I felt that I got to have a real relationship in high school, when all I ever heard from those who were older than me, those queer folks who had come before and fought for a world where I could live openly and honestly, was that queer adolescence was a time of insufferable isolation and that love wouldn't come until I was at least thirty. I never thought I could wait that long.

Standing in my kitchen in exactly the position in which I received the text message, I recalled how Jon always smelled strangely like lilac, which made him feel immediately familiar, as I spent my summers in childhood cutting lilac blossoms in my backyard and placing them in vases and mason jars throughout the house, our open windows circulating the scent of lilac from room to room, pressing it into each crook and corner and even deep into the couch cushions—so that come December you'd swear you could still smell it there by burying your face deep into the crevices. It was a smell so large that living there was like inhabiting a bloom of pale violet, and I knew it made my mom happy, which made me happy.

Jon had made me happy in that same innocent, all-encompassing way. I recalled how I felt when he showed up at a talk I gave before a group of Christians about growing up gay in the church—how he sat in the back of the room beside my mom, beaming and extending his thumbs up as if they were pointing toward heaven, how his smile contained everything that was good and right in the world, and how it quashed my anxiety. I recalled how he sat down at the piano and serenaded me with John Denver while his friends laughed in kitchen, the smell of baking brownies wafting over the threshold and into the dimly lit living room. I recalled how he wore my cross and how it pressed into my chest through our shirts whenever we hugged, and how he always tasted of peppermint Altoids, a flavor I once detested but came to cherish.

I recalled the times we talked about going to my prom and how I felt when we committed to calling one another "boyfriend," the decision made over the phone while I was in bed recovering from wisdom-teeth extraction surgery, my mouth full of blood as I lay under a quilt and beneath a James Dean poster, grinning through the post-surgery haze at my bedroom door, eagerly anticipating my mom's next check-in so that I could let her know, and how she scolded me for using the phone so soon after surgery but couldn't stop herself from mirroring my goofy expression.

But the most vivid memory of all that I revisited had occurred just the night before—at my eighteenth birthday party. Jon needed to leave early, so he had asked if I would accompany him to his car. The crickets had buzzed as we sat on the car's hood, a sea of wispy clouds perched above our heads like a gilded crown.

Sitting side-by-side, leaning our backs against the car's windshield, we had looked up to the night sky in search of those few stars that shone bright enough to break through the suburban light pollution. Suspended in silence like flies in amber, neither of us had wanted to say goodbye—ever since he had come out to his parents, our meetings had become less frequent and increasingly short.

After a period of silence, Jon had turned to me and said, "You know what? No matter what gets thrown our way, I just know we're going to be all right."

I had bit my lip, tearing off the tiniest piece of skin with a canine.

"I love you, Chris," he had continued. "I can't wait to celebrate all of the rest of your birthdays with you and, someday, share you with my family."

Turning to face him, I had found that he was crying. I would've done anything to make it so that our relationship wasn't bittersweet for him.

"Same here," I had said, sighing. The crickets played on.

"Well, you'd better get home," I had continued. And then, before I could stop myself, I had added: "I can't wait until we don't have to be a secret anymore." I had said it louder than I intended to—it was meant to be an under-my-breath remark—but he nodded knowingly.

As he so often did, Jon had lied to his parents so that he could come to the party, telling them he was hanging out with his friend Claire. But he'd neglected to tell Claire this, and his parents had run into her at the grocery store. They had returned home and searched his stuff, finding a letter he'd written to me, and said the relationship needed to end.

And so it did. With that recognition, all of those memories were swept away, all of them, and I was alone with the realization that it was actually over. I was shattered.

It seemed impossible, a grievous betrayal—after years of feeling different, isolated, alone, years of being the only queer kid at my school and in my church, I had convinced myself that nobody had ever felt the way that I'd felt, that nobody ever would, and that things would never change. And then I *met* someone who had felt the way I'd felt, someone who had changed everything, had fixed everything. . . . But the universe, without even asking, had snatched it away, like so many other things before it—my father, my church, the friends who abandoned me when I came out—and I was once again afraid, empty, alone. I could not conceive of the possibility that I might experience that kind of intimacy again; it came, it went, and I was left behind.

In that moment it felt worse to know that it was possible to be loved; thinking it was out of the question allowed for a kind of resignation, an acceptance of the condition of things. But this, this knowing, was so much worse. I had tasted something delicious and wanted to eat nothing else, only to abruptly develop a life-threatening allergy; a condition of inexorable swelling that, without intervention, would suffocate me.

I couldn't breathe and, in a rare moment of unbridled anger, threw my phone across the kitchen. It bounded off the sink faucet, pinging as it landed beside the soap dish. I ran downstairs to my room, locking the copper doorknob behind me, and climbed into bed.

I shut my eyes and tried to force myself into an exhausted sleep. Upstairs, my mom plucked the remaining candles from the blue-frosted cake she had baked me, returning them one by one to their box.

—⁘—

I spent most of the day of our breakup—a Sunday—in my bedroom, reflecting on our relationship. Though we had rarely disagreed, our affair had been rife with high school melodrama. While my family had met him on several occasions, I had no idea what his family was like. He was always paranoid that they would discover our relationship, and I did everything I could to be patient, understanding, and flexible. But when sneaking around his parents got in the way of our seeing one another or even talking on the phone, it crushed me. I began to develop a deep-seated anger at the world for cultivating the kinds of views that made this deception necessary.

Lying in my bed, I felt myself getting angrier and angrier—at his parents and their backward beliefs, at the institutions that perpetuated and enabled them, and at myself for feeling so helpless in the face of them.

The next morning, I walked into my one class at high school—math, a subject I struggled with and was thus too afraid to take at the community college—and tried to play it cool. Sitting in a class of nearly forty students, I tried to focus on the lesson. My aversion to the subject didn't exactly help, but even if it had been my civics class, I doubt it would've mattered. I could only focus on the possibility that I'd never see my boyfriend again and the feeling of injustice that was burning a hole in my stomach.

A few days later, it was finally the Day of Silence, an event I'd been working toward all year. This was our second year doing it at our high school, Mounds View; a few friends and I had organized one the year prior. But this time we had the people power of a student group behind us since another student and I had cofounded Mounds View's first-ever Gay-Straight Alliance. Our first meeting had drawn over forty students, and we'd been gaining momentum all year.

In the lead-up to this year's event, we tried to be cautious and diplomatic. The year before we'd been very aggressive, and the pushback from some students and parents in the district had been loud and suppressive. In anticipation of our second attempt, I wrote the following announcement and distributed it among the faculty and staff:

> You may have seen a sign or two lining the Mounds View halls announcing the upcoming "Day of Silence" this April 13th. If you have never heard of The Day of Silence previously, allow me to do my best to briefly explain its purpose. According to dayofsilence.org, "The Day of Silence, a project of the Gay, Lesbian and Straight Education Network (GLSEN) in collaboration with the United States Student Association (USSA), is a student-led day of action where those who support making anti-LGBT (lesbian, gay, bisexual, transgender) bias unacceptable in schools take a day-long vow of silence to recognize and protest the discrimination and harassment— in effect, the silencing—experienced by LGBT students and their allies." This day is not about debating the morality of

one's sexuality; rather, it is about the morality of equality. All students deserve an equal chance at an education without fear of harassment. Far too often, LGBT students feel silenced in their school environment, and this day is a response to that. The Day of Silence is not meant to be disruptive, and if it is essential to the class that a student speak, then they will. However, any cooperation possible will not only help this day be a success, but also send a powerful message that discrimination and violence are not tolerated in the classroom.

Though I received a lot of support, this message was not heeded by everyone. On the day itself, a former math teacher of mine, who was a devout Christian, displayed an anti-gay Bible verse on his blackboard, as well as statistics asserting that the life expectancy of gay men is less than that of their heterosexual peers. When I heard of this, I reported it to the administration and was promised that it would be taken care of. It was not.

There was also a lot of conflict among students. A group led a prayer vigil outside the school, calling it "The Day of Truth." A football teammate picked a fight with my younger brother, saying he was a fag just like his older brother. A former classmate of mine wore a shirt that read: "Silly faggot—dicks are for chicks!" Though we reported him, he did not face any consequences.

I was furious at the administration's tolerance of these events. *What if it had been a comparably derogatory slam at women, black people, or the disabled?* I wondered. *Surely, they'd have done something.*

I felt my anger over this mount and meet up with the fury and frustration I was feeling over the end of my relationship and the beliefs that had caused it. Sympathetic adults told me that things would improve with time—that I just had to wait it out—but I didn't want to "get over it." My frustrations fermented, and I began to see everyone as homophobic until they proved otherwise.

I had largely checked out of Mounds View life by the time my graduation approached. About a month after the Day of Silence, it was time for our senior retreat, and I was wholly unenthusiastic about it. As the day began, I turned to my friend Heidi and said, "Man, I don't even know why I'm going to this. Like, do I really want to have to hang out with Nate Beske all day and hear all about how awesome high school was for him?"

I didn't really mean Nate specifically; it was more what Nate symbolized. He was athletic, funny, well-dressed, and very popular. He had proudly headed up the Republican side of Mounds View's mock presidential debates the year before and sped off every day at 3:05 p.m. in an expensive car. Life seemed to come so easy to him, and he came to represent everything I resented about my high school years—the ways in which I felt marginalized, abnormal, inferior, unvalued.

The retreat was exactly what I had expected: a day of reminiscing about the glories of those for whom high school had been an idyllic experience. I gritted my teeth and stuck to the periphery with some of my friends.

To close the retreat, there was an open mic sharing section. I sat there as peer after peer went forward and offered inspirational reflections on what our futures might hold, peppered with anecdotes that exemplified how much they would miss their classmates and how they would always treasure the experiences they had all shared. My stomach got tighter and tighter as I heard them tell of everything I had missed out on because I'd felt so unsafe there.

I decided I should say something. Because I had spent the last two years largely away from Mounds View, some people knew I was gay, but many still didn't. I was half-in and half-out of the closet, and I needed to step out all the way. So I tried to work up the nerve to stand up, but as soon as I thought I was close to doing so, someone else rose to use the microphone.

"Remember that time someone released geese in the hallway?" someone said, and everyone laughed.

"Remember that time Neil streaked during the sectionals game halftime?" More laughter.

"Remember when someone pulled the fire alarm and we all had to stand outside, and then we had a dance party in the parking lot?" *No, I don't.*

Finally, I could not wait any longer. I stood up and quickly walked to the front, ready for a battle. I needed people to hear me out, whether they wanted to or not.

"I know many of you know who I am, but some of you might be surprised that I still go here," I said. "No, I didn't transfer to Irondale." A few laughs, and some confused faces.

"Well, you probably don't know this, but I decided to take most of my classes at a community college because I didn't feel safe here," I said. "See, I'm gay, and I was too afraid to face the people who I thought were judging me for being different." I spotted Nate in the crowd but avoided his stare. *Fuck him and everyone here like him,* I thought.

"The advice I'd like to offer is that I hope none of you will allow fear to dictate the decisions you make," I said, my mouth dry and my forehead soaking. "I don't regret my choice, but listening to you all today, I can't help but feel like I missed out on a lot because I was scared. So, you know, don't be scared of who you are or what other people will think of you. Life's too short for that."

I finished, relieved to have finally addressed what had felt, to me, like an elephant in the room for four years. I no longer cared what they thought, and I also felt a lot less angry. For a moment there was nothing—the room was motionless—and then, a single person shot from his seat like a firework.

It was Nate.

Suddenly, my entire graduating class leapt to their feet, as if Nate had given them permission to do so, and the room exploded with applause. I was astonished.

After, Nate approached me and gave me a hug. "I'm not sure I agree with you, dude, but that was brave."

Nate Beske had hugged me. *What alternate universe have I stepped into?* I thought. Though I didn't know it then, years later we would reconnect and he'd become a trusted friend and confidante.

The next day I accepted the Lutheran Student Award scholarship from an LGBTQ organization, and in my acceptance speech I told that story as a cautionary tale against putting people in boxes and counting them as enemies when they might be allies. I was honored for my work as a queer activist in Christian circles—for the vigils I attended during the Evangelical Lutheran Church in America's vote on sexual orientation and ministry, for leading a protest of a reparative-therapy conference, for the LGBTQ Christian panels I sat on that drew the ire of Westboro Baptist Church, and for the dialogue I facilitated within the Lutheran Church on issues of human sexuality.

But though I pledged to continue my activism—I was headed to a Lutheran college, where I hoped to study to become a minister, thinking that I could draw on my experiences of being "othered" in order to work with those on the margins of society—my religious beliefs were on shaky ground. Nate had restored my faith in humanity, diminished after years of experiencing dehumanization for being gay—but my days of believing the Christian tenets were numbered.

5

Unholier Than Thou: Saying Goodbye to God

That God does not exist, I cannot deny.
That my whole being cries out for God, I cannot forget.

—Jean-Paul Sartre

After years of working to reconcile being gay with being a Christian, I entered Augsburg College ready for a fresh start on solid ground. It was to be a time of spiritual growth that would set my call to ministry. I expected college to be difficult but merely in the way that college is difficult for many others—the late-night cram sessions followed by early-morning exams, the growing pains of newfound independence, and the difficulty of discerning which peer pressures to concede.

I didn't expect that I would stop believing in God altogether.

It's hard to put my finger on the demise of my belief in God. There was no moment of revelation, no neat and tidy bookend to the years of belief that followed my initial conversion. The conclusion of my Christian faith was a gradual process; it was something that happened in increments as a result of careful thought and investigation.

I suppose it started in my Religion 100 class, the first of two required religion classes at Augsburg. One of our earliest assignments was a project in which we were asked to define our "canon." After learning about the process through which biblical texts became canonized—something I'd been ignorant of beforehand—we were invited to define our own personal canon of texts. I listed songs, movies, poems, and books that had been especially influential. Flannery O'Connor, Sufjan Stevens, Pär Lagerkvist, Tom Waits, and a Kevin Smith film all made the list. I relished the project, and it was only after I submitted it that I realized I hadn't included the Bible.

It's revealing to me now that I listed Lagerkvist, whose Nobel Prize–winning novel, *Barabbas*, was among my favorite literary works at the time. That book, which imagines the life of the man who was released by the Romans in place of Jesus, was Lagerkvist's way of elucidating his lifelong struggle over his lack of faith and inability to believe in Jesus. Though I didn't know it at the time, Barabbas's story was my own.

I wanted to believe in God. I wanted to love Jesus and participate in His fellowship of believers. I looked to many Christians as pillars of goodness, and I wanted to emulate their compassion and social justice ethic. Sure, there were Christians promoting hate, but I'd met few people more dedicated to repairing the world and helping those in need than the Christians I knew. I earnestly believed that, to be like them, I needed to believe in their God. It seemed to be a package deal, but I was much more invested in the positive, human-affirming ethics and the community aspect of it than I was in the theism.

It was kind of heartbreaking, then, when I realized that I no longer believed in God. With the same kind of recognition I experienced when I finally put the word *gay* onto the feelings I'd had for most of my life, it eventually hit me that I was an atheist. It was as if I had come home from an especially long week at work to find out that God had packed up His things and moved out days before without leaving a forwarding address, and I'd just been too busy to notice His absence.

I didn't come to the personal conclusion that God probably didn't exist because I was angry. It wasn't merely a reaction to the problems I saw in many religious beliefs and communities, or to the negative experiences I'd had—I had already made my peace with my past and saw that religious communities were making progress on addressing dehumanizing beliefs and practices. Rather, it was a conclusion I came to through intellectual and personal consideration. As I studied religion, I took a step back and reflected on the arguments for and against the existence of God, and was underwhelmed by the evidence. Recalling my nontheism in childhood, it suddenly seemed odd that I had adopted a theistic worldview after not having had one in my youth. It became apparent that believing in a divine force simply didn't resonate with my experiences or how I understood the world.

I had thought that my negative experiences—all those years of believing that God was ignoring my pleas to be rid of the burden of being gay, the years I spent hating myself for who I was—were God's way of helping me understand the experience of suffering; that they were preparation for pastoral work in solidarity with the marginalized and disenfranchised. I wanted to help others, and the people I knew who helped others the most were pastors. But what I didn't fully understand then was that my desire to help others and be in a community existed apart from the theological claims of Christianity, which had never sat as easily with me. After I was encouraged by my college professors to critically examine the underlying desires that initially propelled me into Christianity, I left the Church.

I remember vividly those first college nights that followed my awareness of my atheism; how I would climb into bed after an overlong study session or a hushed dorm-room party, close my eyes and have to quash my instinct to pray, and how it felt like extinguishing a cigarette before it was actually finished—unnatural, premature.

Sometimes I would try to pray anyway, just to see if it still "worked," like the way I sometimes pick up the trombone to see if I can still play all these years later. But praying felt like an act, so wholly phony, so I put it in the back of the closet to collect dust. Prayer became like that unplayed trombone or a phantom limb, something I once used regularly but now am not sure was ever mine.

Letting go of God was difficult. Even as I began to step up my antireligious rhetoric in college, I privately mourned God. I wanted to believe and was disappointed in my inability to do so. I missed Him—and the community and ethical commitments that came along with Him.

I didn't jump into calling myself an atheist right away. I wasn't ready to renounce God publicly—many of my social relationships had been formed through my participation in Christian communities. And I didn't really like the word, either. Why would I call myself an atheist? It seemed to arrogantly declare, "Yes, I know definitively that God does not exist."

On the other hand, I wanted to feel the kind of assuredness that Christianity had given me, and a complete rejection of organized religion gave me that. I looked for religious demons everywhere. Suddenly Michele Bachmann, a Minnesota state senator who believed that global warming was a myth and that gay marriage was the worst thing that could happen to our society, came to represent all Christians in my mind. (I relished pointing out her bizarre beliefs in a column for my college newspaper.) I sought out any opportunity to point to religion and say, "See! Look how bad it is." When you're looking for garbage, you'll find it. It became easy to notice the flaws and miss the merits.

In an impressive bit of internal dissonance, I simultaneously set out on a quasi-quest—a kind of spiritual seeking—but I was quickly overwhelmed by the choices. There were so many religions, and each offered something equally exciting and different. I wanted it all! I wanted Jesus and Buddha and Confucius and Darwin. But I felt the victim of the medieval dictum that "every choice is a renunciation"—that choosing to follow one path meant that I had to forsake every other. After all, wasn't that part of why I left Christianity? Because it had felt, to me, limited in its scope—a definitive statement to an unanswerable question.

This short exploration was half-hearted; I had already made up my mind that I was an atheist. It was like going into the fitting room at the mall and trying on fifteen different shirts while knowing you don't have the money to pay for any of them. I was going through the motions, but I wasn't really making progress.

Even as I tried on different identities, I began to step up my antireligious behavior, arrogantly rolling my eyes at anyone with a semblance of certainty. Christianity became my special target. I decided that after our break-up I did *not* want to be friends.

This tension was reflected in my college religion papers. I walked the line between denouncing religion and trying to rescue it from itself, for myself. *Maybe Christianity can be resurrected*, I thought, *if I just defend it enough.* I read the writings of progressive theologians with a quiet resentment, jealous of their ability to modernize Christianity but still retain a belief in God. I was mad at myself for not being able to believe—after years of struggling to reconcile my belief in God with my queer identity (and eventually succeeding), it felt unfair to have done so in vain.

Some theologians and religious practitioners tell me that dry spells happen and that perhaps I gave up on God too quickly, but years later I am surer than ever that I don't believe in God, and struggle to recall why I did in the first place. To be honest, the question no longer intrigues me—I'm much too interested in the complexities of being human to spend much time thinking about anything beyond that.

However, in the years immediately following my departure from Christianity, that was anything but true. I was frustrated and unsettled, and I found myself once again wrestling with the tension of not fitting into a traditional paradigm.

After years of denying my own instincts and questioning the validity of central aspects of who I am, my identity became structured in response to other people's identities. Though I didn't realize it at the time, I was trying to affirm the conclusions I had reached by working to persuade others to be convinced in kind. If I instilled doubt in another, my own skepticism felt more legitimate. And though my atheism wasn't born of anger, I found myself resisting others' religious expressions with a previously unfamiliar degree of annoyance—especially at their most reverent.

The day after the Interstate 35W Mississippi River Bridge collapsed without warning during rush hour, I stood with a group of friends near the wreckage, where we gathered for an impromptu vigil. I couldn't believe that this massive structure—a bridge I often used to get from my apartment, which was a few blocks away from our vigil, to my job at a folk-music school just across the river—was no more.

Just like that, it disappeared.

I was at work when it happened. I heard an unusual loud noise, looked out the window, and saw a cloud of dust. Curious, I locked up the school and wandered down the street. As I approached the bridge, the scene was unlike anything I had ever seen before—police cars and fire trucks formed a blockade around both sides of the bridge, and dust clouded the air. A swarm of people were hugging and crying, and everything was roped off by police tape. I ran into friends and felt relieved that they were okay. I immediately tried to call everyone I knew in the area, but because so many people were trying to use their cell phones, no one could get a call out. So we just stood there, numb and horrified, and took solace in one another's company.

Surrounded by friends a day later, I felt sadness for those who had died mixed with gratitude that the casualties had been few. But I was also annoyed—in the wake of death and destruction, I couldn't abide the prayers I overheard. I thought that praying was futile at best, and inappropriate and disrespectful at worst.

"This is bullshit," I mumbled as I listened to a friend pray aloud.

As I surveyed the empty space where there was once a bridge, I tried to pretend that I wasn't filling the empty space that once held my belief in God with resentment. The brown waters of the Mississippi continued their journey to the Atlantic, but I was frozen in place.

I didn't believe in God anymore, but I didn't know how to be anything but angry about it. He had disappeared, and all I felt was absence.

—⁂—

Despite my conflicted views on religion, college was a largely positive experience. I jumped at the wealth of opportunities I had to learn and grow. In my second year at Augsburg, I spent the month of January in El Salvador—a special treat for a lifelong Minnesotan, to be sure—on a study-abroad trip through Augsburg's Center for Global Education. I was ecstatic; for months leading up to the trip, it was all I could talk about.

The dozen or so students participating in the course spent the first chunk of the program in the capital city of San Salvador. We were carefully guarded by the trip chaperones. Only once did a few of us manage to escape their watchful eyes long enough to wander the city unsupervised for a brief hour.

There was something about the tropical heat and the chaotic streets that made me see things out of the corner of my eye that weren't really there. But it became immediately clear that one thing I wasn't imagining was the stark economic inequality in El Salvador. People with money seemed to be hiding behind walls, white halls, and armed guards, content to ignore the rampant poverty just beyond their landscaped yards. I didn't understand how they could just pretend it wasn't there.

Though my childhood was meager by some standards, I'd never even seen economic disparity like I saw that day—garbage cans ablaze, dispensing smog and haze; children unwatched and unclothed, sitting atop self-made stacks of dirt and newspaper; trash piled so high that it obscured the barbed wire and broken glass adorning nearly every fence and wall; mansions on one hillside, cardboard shacks on the next. It rattled me, and I was actually relieved when one of the chaperones managed to reach us by phone and request that we come back to the hostel.

Later that day, the group piled in the van to visit La Divina Providencia, the site where Monsignor Óscar Romero was assassinated. I was wearing shorts to compensate for the heavy Salvadoran heat. Growing up in Minnesota, shorts became a treasured commodity I only got to bust out of the furthest depths of my closet for those beautiful and brief summer months. The rest of the year was cold enough that exposed limbs were a rare sight; thick pajamas were required to make winter nights tolerable. For much of my life my legs spent very little time absorbing the light of day, and I could go for weeks without seeing the stalk of wheat and Bible verse I'd had inked on my right calf in high school.

Sure enough, someone in the van noticed the tattoo on my leg and asked me about it. I became flushed with hot embarrassment, reddening my already sunburned face.

"Oh, that? Yeah, I got that back when I was still a Christian," I muttered. Embarrassment washed over me—*there it was*, I thought, *another reminder of those years I'd spent as a deluded fool.*

"What does it mean? What's the verse?" my friend inquired.

"It's Jesus speaking," I said through gritted teeth. "It goes: 'I tell you for certain that unless a grain of wheat falls to the ground and dies, it will remain only one grain. But if it dies, it bears much fruit.'

"Or something like that," I added dismissively so as to seem disinterested.

"Wow, that's beautiful. But do you regret it, since you're, you know, not a Christian anymore?"

I exhaled loudly and complained to those seated nearby about just how stupid it was that I got the tattoo shortly before I stopped believing in God. It was as if I'd known deep down that my belief was already in its sunset—as if I was desperately clinging onto its vestige with a bold and permanent statement, as if to say: *There, self, now you* can't *get out of it.* I added that no one under the age of twenty should be allowed to make the decision to alter his or her skin. My friends smiled tightly, mouths closed, and I realized I was offending them. I decided I didn't care. They knew I didn't believe in God, so they shouldn't have been surprised. If I was expected to tolerate their religious proclamations, then they needed to accept my irreligious rants.

Still, I trend toward peacemaking over rabble-rousing, so I started to get anxious about my comments. *Fine,* I thought, *under the rug it goes. We just won't talk about our differences, for the sake of "getting along." They don't want to hear what matters to me, and I don't care to know what matters to them.*

I changed the subject to our impending visit to Monsignor Romero's assassination site. I idolized Romero. Here was a man unafraid to take a stand for what was right. With a camera, I captured every Salvadoran mural, painting, and icon emblazoned with Romero's image. My primary impetus to study in El Salvador was my fascination with Romero and the incredible story of his life.

Appointed Archbishop of San Salvador in 1977—to the satisfaction of the corrupt Salvadoran government—Romero was initially a conservative Catholic leader largely uninterested in politics. After the assassination of a personal friend, Romero underwent a transformation and began to speak out against the grueling Salvadoran poverty, government-sanctioned assassination and torture, and other rampant injustices. He started to draw international attention to the horrors going on in El Salvador, citing his newfound allegiance to liberation theology as his incentive to speak out against El Salvador's human rights violations. He spoke too loudly for some and was assassinated just three years after his appointment.

At the time, I failed to connect the dots between Romero's religious motivations and his brave deeds. Somehow, I managed to divorce the religious assertions of the archbishop from his actions. *He would've done those things anyway,* I justified. *He was just speaking the language of his context. His actions, with or without the religious motivations behind them, are what matter here.* That he was a religious man and that his actions were deeply rooted in his personal religious convictions were things I didn't want to think about.

We arrived at the site, and the chatter in the van died down. We exited the vehicle and were met by a middle-aged woman with a loose-fitting white blouse that occasionally caught the whisper of a Salvadoran breeze. She introduced herself as Rosaline and explained that she would be giving us a tour of the site. Beginning at Romero's living quarters, we followed behind her. Producing no sound but the crunch of gravel beneath our feet, we listened with more attention than we usually gave our professors as she shared details about the history of La Divina Providencia and Romero's involvement.

Before long, Rosaline stopped us at the front of the church and invited us inside. The cool air of the sanctuary was a welcome respite from the Salvadoran sun. Light filtered in through the large windows, and the sound of our footsteps echoed against the walls as we timidly entered the room and took seats in the pews.

Slowly and solemnly, Rosaline informed us that this was the actual location of Romero's assassination. She detailed the day of his death: how several men had pulled up outside the small church while Romero was at the pulpit; how they shot at him through the open doors and drove off; how he bled and quickly died. I looked through the open doors and wondered why Romero hadn't shut them. *He had known that his life was in danger,* I thought. *Why hadn't he guarded himself a little more closely?*

"Just weeks before he was murdered, Monsignor Romero said, 'If God accepts the sacrifice of my life, may my death be for the freedom of my people.'"

I looked up at the ceiling of the church as Rosaline spoke in a thick accent.

She continued quoting Romero: "'A bishop will die, but the Church of God, which is the people, will never perish. If they kill me, I shall arise in the Salvadoran people.'"

I was breathless.

After a moment of silence, our guide notified us that Romero had been mid-Homily when he was shot. In true religious narrative form, Romero was actually preaching about how he knew that he was a marked man but that what was "right" mattered more than what was safe or comfortable.

At the end of her talk, Rosaline informed us that this Homily had revolved around a verse of Scripture. She asked if she could share it with us. We nodded all at once without saying a word.

"In the words of our Lord and Savior Jesus Christ," she began, "'I tell you for certain that unless a grain of wheat falls to the ground and dies, it will remain only one grain. But if it dies, it bears much fruit.'"

I shut my eyes tight and bowed my head toward the ground so as not to feel the gazes of those who had been sitting near me in the van. *No fucking way*, I thought. *You've got to be kidding me.*

Chance is a funny thing and it is easily mistaken for portent. A birthday check from your grandparents arrives at just the right moment, saving you from a late rent fee. You reconnect with a person you met a year before and suddenly see him or her in a new way. You pray for health and just like that—like a miracle— your cold is gone. But, tempting as it may be to think otherwise, I don't believe that the universe maintains any preordained or intelligent order. My best guess is that such lucky occurrences are, well, just that.

Yet as I sat in a Salvadoran church smarting with the memory of my own sardonic commentary, sentimentality washed over me. I felt such a longing to *believe* again—to see this moment as a Gift, as an Instruction, as Fruition. I fought this idea and my resulting emotions, biting my lip so that I wouldn't cry. It didn't work, so I swallowed hard and tasted blood. Turning away from the spot where Romero bled, I walked out into the sunlight and out into a city still suffering inequalities that Romero gave his life to redress.

I don't know why I felt I needed that episode to be intentionally orchestrated in order to cull significance from it—it was significant on its own merit. I imagine that a desire for purpose is innate for many of us. We presuppose that learning occurs within larger, cosmic narrative structures. Things *matter* because there is an implicit reason behind their occurrence, and it is our job to discern the organic meaning within. Constellating and creating our own sense of meaning from such moments can feel insufficient; discovering some preordained answer seems more compelling. In that moment I wanted to be handed a fate, not fashion my own.

But soon enough it was as if none of what had happened in Romero's church had ever transpired. Instead of honestly grappling with and responding to the immensity of that moment, I tossed it aside. I was mortified with myself for having looked for a sign of God, and the coincidence was relegated to the camp of charming curiosity. Religion—and my postreligious search for values and meaning—remained as dead to me as Oscar Romero, entombed in stone and unreachable.

—∿∿—

With my El Salvador trip finished, I set to finishing my degree.

Augsburg's philosophy is that education does not just take place in the classroom, and students are required to participate in off-campus community service work in their first semester. I volunteered with an organization called the Campus Kitchen at Augsburg College, a satellite of the national Campus Kitchen Project. CKAC recovered unused food from the campus cafeteria and distributed it to hunger-relief agencies in the area. I became enamored with the work of CKAC in my first semester at Augsburg and looked for opportunities to move into leadership; when a slot opened up on the Leadership Team, I was thrilled to be invited. I requested the chance to lead the volunteer shift I'd been trained on, a weekly visit to deliver food to the Brian Coyle Community Center.

Just blocks from school, BCCC served the Cedar-Riverside neighborhood, the most densely populated area of Minnesota, with nearly two thousand apartment units in a two-block area. Cedar-Riverside is home to Riverside Plaza, immortalized as the building in the opening sequence of *The Mary Tyler Moore Show*. Designed to be a utopian complex accommodating people from the highest of incomes to the lowest, today it primarily consists of subsidized housing. Numerous students at my school (who mostly refused to leave campus in anything but a car with locked doors for fear of being "shanked") not-so-lovingly referred to Riverside Plaza as "The Crack Stacks" and "The Slum in the Sky." (Those same individuals, most of whom had cars on campus, would go a few extra miles to avoid the closest Target, which they dubbed "Targhetto.")

I was embarrassed by how many of my classmates wrote off an entire group of people. Yes, there was significantly more violent crime in that area than in other parts of Minneapolis, and it was important to be careful there. Crime is a reality in Cedar-Riverside, and that isn't changing: a year after I graduated and stopped volunteering there, an Augsburg student volunteer was shot and killed leaving BCCC. Still, I rarely felt uncomfortable walking or biking through Cedar-Riverside. There were times when I felt slightly unsafe and quickened my pace, but those times were few. The reason I was never the victim of such violence may have been pure and random luck, but I also believe that the fears many had about the neighborhood were overblown—if they had gotten to know more of the community's residents, they might've thought differently.

This idea that relationality has a transformative impact was one reason I so enjoyed working at BCCC. I wasn't just interested in dropping off some food once a week and patting myself on the back for doing my part. I wanted relationships with the people who frequented BCCC, to invite them to share their stories and to share my own. It was less about my coming in to "do something nice" and more about mutually enriching relationships between those serving and those being served. Service work should never be a one-way street—otherwise it's tempting to imagine yourself as a hero and those you are assisting as in need of saving. These were people who were just like me but who had experienced a different

set of life circumstances. Knowing that, I hoped to establish relationships of mutual care and concern with people that so many of
my classmates seemed to ignore.

Sure enough, I started to become an active member of the
BCCC community. I dropped by to say hi when I was in the area,
attended neighborhood meetings, and stayed late after some volunteer shifts to spend more time talking. I became well acquainted
with the lives of those I served and began to better understand, in
particular, the challenges faced by Somali immigrants in Minneapolis, who were the majority in Cedar-Riverside. When a young
girl with big brown eyes and a striking red head scarf vividly described her first encounter with snow, I felt like I was experiencing Minnesota winter for the first time. When a mother with one
child in her arm and two running around her feet thanked me
for helping her son with his math homework, I admitted that he
actually knew more about the subject than I did. When I missed
a week due to a bad cold, everyone grinned at my return and told
me how much they had missed and worried about me. We became
invested in one another's lives, and we taught one another how to
be together. They even tried to coach me on some rudimentary
Somali but always playfully chided me for not sounding forceful
enough. "You sound too Minnesotan!" they'd say with a chuckle.
(And they were right.)

But when it came to matters of religious life, I disengaged.
I knew I should not bring pork to BCCC, and I knew why. But
I avoided discussing it because it had to do with religion. Some
of my antireligious friends would make jokes about me bringing
pepperoni pizza on my shift, and I would crack a weak smile and
change the subject.

Now here was a new tension. It was one thing to mock my
own religious past, because it was mine, but the jokes about the
religious beliefs of the people I served at BCCC started to make me

uncomfortable. These were people I cared about, and their beliefs mattered deeply to them.

One day, I stayed a bit later than usual, caught up in conversation with a group of BCCC regulars. Gradually all but one trickled away, leaving me alone with a young woman I had spoken to a handful of times. She was petite but her presence filled the room— she spoke rapidly and precisely. A few plates of food scraps sat on the table in front of us as we quizzed one another on the details of our lives.

After some talk of how terribly the Minnesota Timberwolves had been playing that year and which local politicians we were voting for, she paused and looked down at the nearly empty plate in front of her and took a deep breath.

"You know, some days I'm really afraid to go out in public because of how I dress. I just get tired of dealing with the stares and jeers my hijab elicits," she said, barely audible.

We were both silent. I heard a shout from down the hall that signaled that the gymnasium was closing and all basketballs should be returned to the equipment closet.

"It's not exactly the same thing, but I think I can empathize a little," I said before I could stop myself.

She looked up. Her face showed that she was curious about how I, a white guy who looked like every other young Minnesota hipster who used the Greenway (a bicycle freeway) to get around, might relate.

"Sometimes I get really nervous about the looks I get when I'm holding another man's hand in public." I wasn't sure how she would respond to this new information. I wasn't really out to anyone at BCCC—I assumed that, because many of them were religious, it would be an issue.

She smiled, and I realized I hadn't taken a breath in the last minute.

"When I'm afraid of how others might receive me," she said, leaning in, her elbows sliding across the table, "it is my belief in Allah that gives me strength."

She wasn't proselytizing; she was sharing her beliefs. She hadn't asked for clarification about what I had said, hadn't condemned me; she hadn't even blinked.

"May I ask you: what gives you strength when you get such looks, or when someone says something disparaging about you because of who you are?" She looked me in the face, her eyes warm and inviting.

I froze. I looked down at her elbows and noticed that they were fixed in place.

"Um, do you know when this place shuts down for the night?" I asked, shifting my head to the left, unable to look her in the eye. If I were being honest, I would've said, "I'm shutting down this conversation for the night."

Her religious beliefs were integral to her identity, and she had opened a door for us to discuss the things that mattered to us both with candor and honesty. Yet I couldn't even bring myself to speak up when some of my friends mocked the religious convictions of Muslims I worked with at BCCC—so how could I discuss religion with her? I was afraid to open up to her—the gulf I imagined between the experiences of a gay atheist and Muslim woman seemed too vast. I decided our values and identities were irrelevant to the work I was there to do and slammed shut the door that she had opened. Rising abruptly, I picked up the plates from the table and grabbed my bike helmet with a fumble, inventing some story about a big paper that was due the next day.

I realize now that I was just as guilty of diminishing many of Cedar-Riverside's residents as my "Targhetto"-fearing peers or those making crass jokes about pepperoni pizza were. My "don't ask, don't tell" approach to working with Minneapolis's Muslim community was inhibiting; my refusal to engage the religious identities of my BCCC colleagues closed me off from countless opportunities to build bridges of understanding and respect with a community I honestly knew very little about, aside from my academic study of Islam. I was in a position to learn from a community that (especially post-9/11) many people—myself included—viewed with fear and suspicion, but I declined. By refusing to open up to them about my own beliefs and experiences, I also denied them the opportunity to learn about me—to really know me and understand the challenges that I faced.

When I refused to engage the full person with those at BCCC, I wasn't living up to my aspiration of empowering individuals and seeing them as deserving of dignity and respect. As a religion major, I was also doing myself, and the subjects I studied at Augsburg, an intellectual injustice by not taking religious identities seriously. And as a friend to the people I worked with at BCCC, I was quarantining myself from the meaty conversations of mutuality.

Years later, I had the opportunity to work with members of the Muslim community in Chicago. At first blush, it once again seemed we had little in common. At one of my first community meetings, I was approached by a young woman who asked why I was there. I told her that I was an atheist looking to learn more about the Muslim community. Her eyes flicked to my right, as if to check with someone if it was all right for me to be there. But her hesitation didn't last long; within minutes, we were gushing over our mutual love for a new Brother Ali song, "Tightrope." In it, Brother Ali—a Muslim rapper from Minnesota—tells the stories of a young Muslim woman who faces discrimination for wearing a headscarf and a closeted gay teenager who is the son of an anti-gay Christian minister. We bonded over how we both felt that the song represented struggles we ourselves had experienced and the parallels between them. By the end of the conversation, she and I had uncovered a lot of common ground between our seemingly disparate identities.

After that conversation, I reflected on how different it was from those I'd had when working with the Somali community in Minneapolis, and how important it was to build that kind of understanding. But back in Minneapolis, I couldn't see that. I was happier to pretend that practiced religion was at best irrelevant or stupid and at worst destructive, and that there was little or nothing to be gained by talking about our different beliefs and experiences. I pedaled away from BCCC a little faster than usual that night, telling myself that my hurry was because the sun was setting and I felt unsafe.

—∞—

That I would feel unsafe at night was, of course, a case of massive self-deception, as I'd actually become a frequent creature of the night—and, on some evenings, a night terror. As college came to an end, more and more nights were carousing, careening affairs.

On one such night, I stormed off into the dark as a friend's laughter echoed behind me, goading me on.

We had spent the evening slamming whiskey and ranting about religion. After several hours of drinking straight from a plastic bottle, I was belligerent. I stumbled through the dark, headed nowhere in particular, moving forward without direction, my friend following close behind.

Eventually, I encountered a church sign. It was small and humble—a wooden frame with chipped red paint housing a glass case. On the other side of the glass, misshapen black letters were unevenly arranged to spell the church's name and that week's sermon title, which championed forgiveness or grace or something equally uplifting. Several letters were missing, and the glass plate was clouded with age.

Without a second's thought, I kicked it in.

Staring down at the broken glass splayed before my feet, I saw fragments of my face staring back at me. I didn't recognize my reflection. I had once been kind and quiet, goofy and gentle—now, my face was splintered, creased with anger and self-righteousness.

I heard my friend laugh, louder and harder and louder and harder until it filled my ears and drowned out everything else. I found a doorway and hurled my body into it, huddling against the ground, weeping and slamming my fist into the concrete. I think he thought I was vomiting.

The next day, as I nursed my hangover, we joked about it. "Maybe a synagogue next time?" he said.

I forced a meager laugh and took a sip of a green sports drink. It didn't cure my hangover, but it was cool and soothing—a momentary relief from the gnawing awareness of my thoughtlessness.

Years later I spent an afternoon wandering through that neighborhood in search of the church I'd defaced. It was a hot day, and by the time I finally found it I was drenched. I stood before the sign, wiping the sweat from my face with my t-shirt. There was a new pane of glass in place, clear as a Minnesota lake, and a new sermon title as well: "If you c n't g0 home, come h re."

I walked over to the doorway and sat down in the shade, running a hand along the ground I once punched.

I knew this church wasn't my home, but I no longer wanted to destroy it.

—w—

Though Augsburg encouraged learning outside the classroom through community service, it wouldn't have been a degree program without classes. As I advanced in my studies, I found myself increasingly conflicted about my approach to religion.

I wrestled with Christian doctrine—from Jesus as the Son of God instead of just an allegorical prophet, to the very existence of an anthropomorphic God as a human invention—in my undergraduate thesis, trying to merge it with the Buddhist notion of *upaya* (or "skillful means") and cast Jesus as a *bodhisattva*, but such attempts were half-hearted. I read selections of it to a Buddhist friend, who gave me a sympathetic look and said that I was at my best when I acted as an unwilling repairman for Christianity.

But I didn't really want to fix Christianity—I *wanted* it to be broken, like it had broken me. If Christianity was unfixable then there was a reason for my suffering. And maybe, if Christianity was so inherently problematic that its theology couldn't be resolved, there was still hope for me to be redeemed. I might be able to best it yet.

Though I was at a Christian school, I studied religion as a sociological phenomenon, with a wall of books and computer monitors shielding me from direct contact with religion as a living, breathing organism. From the ivory tower of my academic library it became easy to disconnect myself from the corporeal body of religion and understand it as merely a problematic concept.

I was beginning to fill the void left by Christianity with my own beliefs: I had accepted that I didn't believe in God and even found inspiration in the thought that, if there was no afterlife, then the here-and-now ought to be appreciated and lived to the fullest. But hating religion and the religious wasn't making me happy. It felt just as wrong as being religious had. But when all you know and all you see in the world is dichotomy, there's no way to be anything other than religious or antireligious.

Years later, I am grateful that this period of internal conflict happened while I was at Augsburg, which works hard to create a safe environment for students to ask tough questions and engage in meaningful work. In many ways, Augsburg helped me reign in my rage and frustration; it served to contain me. Had I been somewhere else, I might have spiraled out of control and been entirely consumed by my negative thoughts and unfocused antitheism. The small, caring environment of peers and professors at Augsburg helped me channel my anger into my academic pursuits and social opportunities, so that even as my personal life became little more than a series of unhealthy behaviors, I was ultimately protected from destroying myself.

Despite all of this, I entered my last semester of college with a grade point average that qualified me for *summa cum laude* honors. To achieve *summa* honors at Augsburg, you not only have to meet the GPA minimum but must also write and defend an essay explaining why you deserve special recognition. For my defense panel I selected an English professor I'd worked with on a research paper about Flannery O'Connor and religion, my sociology of religion professor, and my religion major advisor. But perhaps I should have warned them; I was so caustic, bitter, and resentful about my impending religion degree that I titled the essay "Kissing Ass and Taking Names" and in it disparaged a good deal of my coursework and professors. Was I trying to hurt them? Was this my idea of retribution? Because, surely, the entire edifice of Augsburg was to blame for my situation. If it weren't for them, I wouldn't have this damn degree in religion.

My essay was a smack in the face, and I deserved to be reprimanded. But my professors' compassion and forgiveness eclipsed my childish, spiteful writing. Either they were able to recall moments when I'd been more professional—and more creative—or they understood me better than I did. They knew I was capable of more than a witty title to cover for a brute display of bitterness. They knew I'd come around; they granted me *summa cum laude* and sent me on my way. I decided not to walk at graduation, opting to spend that weekend partying instead.

Where was my pride at what I had accomplished? I had paid for this degree all by myself—juggling multiple jobs, earning academic scholarships, and taking out too many student loans. But instead of celebrating my achievement, I wanted to pretend as if it had never happened.

I was insufferable—at that year's Christmas dinner, my father's mother invited me to say grace in celebration of my new bachelor's degree. Instead of offering a humble and grateful reflection, I gave a lecture on the exclusivism of Christmas and how the Sikh notion of the *langar*, or community meal, was a much better model for the kind of gathering we were having.

Shortly after graduating, I got my first tattoo since getting the stalk of wheat in high school. My choice this time was a bit strange, but let me explain. The capybara has always fascinated me—it is a rodent the size of a boar that spends half its life in aquatic conditions. When I watched a television program that claimed that the Catholic Church classifies the capybara as a fish, I knew I had to get it as a tattoo. According to the program, a pope declared the capybara to be a fish after some puzzled missionaries wrote to him inquiring how to classify the creature. The Church, the show concluded, cannot re-classify the capybara as a rodent today due to the doctrine of the infallibility of the pope. After that, I decided that the capybara was a perfect symbol of the absurdity of religious certainty, and I relished the idea that many Catholics in South America actually ate capybara on Fridays during Lent as if it were a fish! (Later in life I decided to research the veracity of this story but had a difficult time locating its origin.)

See how blindly people follow religious rules? I thought with a smarmy grin as I sat, sweating while a bearded tattoo artist labored over me. *Without even a second thought or a pause to question why they do as they are told. Fools.*

I, on the other hand, was so smart because I continued to question everything around me.

Some good it was doing me. At twenty years old, with a religion degree and experience as a newspaper intern, I felt unemployable and unbalanced. Exhausted from having raced my way through college and constantly working to justify my degree against my own claims of the idiocy of religion, I packed up my things and fled the city for Minnesota's great white north. It was there, during a bitter winter in the isolated deep woods, that I was humbled into understanding how my conflicted enmity toward religion was poisoning my own well.

6

Putting My Money Where
Other People's Mouths Are

The best way to find yourself is to lose yourself in the service of others.

— MAHATMA GANDHI

The snow was so high that I couldn't see out the windows.

I lived in a garden apartment, so being snowed-in felt dramatically claustrophobic. I climbed the stairs to the ground level, running my left hand along the string of lights wrapped around the railing on my way up and holding a shovel in my right. Hesitating with a fingerless glove hovering just above the doorknob, I prepared myself for a blast of subzero wind. With a hearty push the door relented, but only enough for my thin frame to squeeze through. After shoveling a direct path to the car, I located a handle, pried the frozen driver's door open, pressed my left foot into the clutch, and turned the key, hoping the machine would grumble to life. With the sun still below the horizon, I dug my car out from beneath a pile of snow while it sputtered and wheezed. I did this every morning for an entire winter, and not once did the car actually warm up before I arrived at work.

Bemidji is a *cold* spot to be from October to May. I'd never visited Bemidji in the winter before I moved there—I had invested in the radiant warmth of summer, in nights spent near the headwaters of the Mississippi River. My introduction to the area came when a group of friends and I drove out into the rural dusk and pitched our tents at a Mississippi canoe launch just miles from the headwaters. The great American river we had come to see was nothing more than a small, marshy creek, though I wouldn't learn that until the light of morning. We got in late and had to saw apart a fallen tree blocking the dirt road to the launch. When we finally arrived at the site, I climbed out the passenger window—the door was permanently jammed shut—and heard, for the first time in years, near silence. We stumbled through the dark to collect logs and kindling, stubbing our toes but not caring much. All night we sat around the fire we had made, a circle only interrupted when someone would wander off to the tree line to relieve herself or himself, the smoke protecting us from the mosquitoes buzzing just beyond our perimeter. We filled the clearing with our laughter—the Minnesota loons echoing our refrains—and allowed lengthy gaps of stillness to sit comfortably unbroken.

Minneapolis is wonderfully loud and colorful, but after spending several years living in a dorm overlooking the interstate and, later, in a crumbling house overflowing beyond its capacity in the heart of frat row, I was ready for some quiet. I wanted to get away from the hectic life I'd created. College had been a time of overachievement: cochairing the College Democrats, serving on the Campus Kitchen at Augsburg College's leadership team, doing grant-funded research projects, coordinating Residence Life, planning and leading summer camps for high school students, and on and on. After spending my undergraduate years grappling with religion as an embittered former Christian and filling the negative space with any extracurricular activity I could, I was exhausted. I wanted to move to a place where things were simple—where I didn't run into ghosts from my former Christian life that reminded me of the years I spent hating myself for being queer and unable to change it. I was worn out. In an attempt to escape, I had fled to the tiny town of Bemidji, located just shy of the Canadian border, where it took hours of driving on back-country single-lane highways to reach the closest "big city": Fargo, North Dakota.

Bemidji's pace was much slower. Okay, so sometimes it was *too* slow. Having grown accustomed to twenty-four-hour groceries in Minneapolis, my roommate and I often had to race to get to the store in Bemidji before it closed, the sun still out. But I was unable to resist the small-town allure. Every morning my coffee-time companion, the *Bemidji Herald*, was rife with news of the happenings of a town full of plaid-clad lumberjacks and hippies seemingly unaware that the 1960s had passed. Most commonly known for its homage to Paul Bunyan and his companion, Babe the Blue Ox, in the form of giant concrete sculptures of the pair that dwarf the quaint downtown, Bemidji has run with its notoriety. Paul and Babe appear everywhere throughout the town, including in "Paul Bunyan Subs," "Paul Bunyan Broadcasting Company," and "Paul Bunyan Mini Storage." I loved the quiet, charming town so much so that I got a tattoo of Paul and Babe.

Kaitlin—a dear friend who worked with me at a bakery and café in high school and who was one of the people I ran into when the 35W Bridge collapsed—and I decided to move to Bemidji after I graduated from college in December. I found a job with Lutheran Social Services as a direct service professional for adults with developmental disabilities. I wasn't exactly thrilled about it being a Lutheran organization, but when you live in Minnesota—land of lutefisk and home to no less than seven Lutheran colleges and four Lutheran seminaries—Lutherans are kind of inescapable. I learned that the agency, though religiously affiliated, was secular in its work, and so I grudgingly accepted the position. My collection of Paul and Babe paraphernalia wouldn't pay for itself, after all.

It was a job unlike any I'd had before. Washing dishes, waiting tables, slicing deli meat, writing for a Minneapolis newspaper: each had been hard in its own way. But this job wore me out more than anything I'd ever done for the same reason it nourished me—I was working with real people on real challenges, from managing the daily difficulties of living in a community to assisting with basic needs and administering medication.

I've been drawn to serving others for much of my life. As a kid, I delivered Meals on Wheels and volunteered at park cleanups; in high school, I volunteered at a drop-in center for LGBTQ youth. For a class assignment in first grade, I scribbled in crayon that I wanted to be a fireman, a police officer, or a doctor so that I could "help people in trouble." From a young age, I've looked out at a world full of injustice and have wanted to do something to help improve the conditions of other people's lives. When I became a Christian, I couched that desire to help in Christian ethics. Jesus Christ exemplified what I wanted to model: the humble servant who put others first, the foot-washer and crowd-feeder, the man who befriended social outcasts. As I tried to understand my desire to "do good" and where it came from, I decided that I did it because Jesus commanded that we care for the needy. But after I lost the faith, I remembered that I had always tried to do good and help others, and that the desire to act selflessly for others transcends religion. Though I didn't have the words for it at the time, I was beginning to cultivate my Humanistic worldview.

But there's a flipside to service. As those who have done direct-service work often attest, it's quite natural to go in thinking that you're only helping others; but if you're paying attention, you'll recognize that you're equally transformed.

I worked in two assisted-living homes—one in Bemidji and one an hour north in a tiny two-block town called Northome—but it was the one just five minutes from my apartment where I spent most of my time. I'd walk into the Bemidji homes and a warm, comfortable feeling would wash over me, like I was stepping into my own home. There was always coffee in the pot—I came to love and prefer mine without cream or sugar—music playing, conversations going, and chores to join in on. The house buzzed with life. When I came in for my interview with the Bemidji house supervisor, a resident named Rosemary sat nearby and wiggled her long fingers, winked her right eye, and clicked her teeth at me. My new boss suggested she was flirting, and Rosemary clapped and laughed in agreement. From that moment on, I was her preferred caregiver. She spoke often but was usually incoherent, so most of our communication happened through the things we did together. We read books, put together puzzles, and drew in coloring books—her art was far better than mine. Every time I removed her socks and helped her get into bed, Rosemary would ask if I'd had fun with her that day. My answer was always an honest and appreciative "yes."

Harry, half-blind, always asked me to go on walks with him. Though we usually stuck to the neighborhood, sometimes we'd go to the Paul Bunyan Mall—a single-level gathering of shops anchored by a Kmart and a Jo-Ann Fabrics—where he'd push a shopping cart to aid his walking and ask every few seconds if he was about to run into something. Most days, there'd be at least one group of kids in oversized t-shirts and skewed baseball caps who would stare or call out something disrespectful, but Harry always took it in stride. "They're young," I'd say, hopeful. "They'll see the world differently someday."

He loved to ask me questions about my life: "Do you live alone?" "How old are you?" "Do you like ice cream?"—though that last one was often a ploy to talk me into buying us Dairy Queen ice cream (something that required very little convincing).

Pete was tougher to get to know. Prone to violent outbursts, he liked to keep to himself most of the time. Sometimes he'd come

into the living room to blast the first twenty-five seconds of El-
ton John's "Crocodile Rock" with his battery-powered boombox
at full volume before starting over again at the beginning (I still
can't listen to that song). But Pete and I had our moments, too. On
a randomly warm day in April, my supervisor suggested I make
hamburgers and cook them on the grill out back. I'm a clueless
cook, and they came out terrible; nervous about undercooking
them, I wound up burning the burgers two-thirds of the way to
the middle of each patty. Serving the charred burgers, I felt embarrassed and offered the residents the option of something else,
but Pete looked up from his plate and chortled, indicating that he
wanted more. I asked him if he was sure and he put up his hand,
covered in baked beans, holding up two fingers to let me know to
keep the burgers coming. I'd never seen him laugh and smile so
much and, for the first time, he gave me a hug and spoke directly
to me: "Thank you."

It was a job, yes, but it functioned like a family. The mantra
among staff was "this is a job, not a friendship," but everyone who
worked there knew that was an unintentional lie. The staff and cli-
ents had to embrace one another's quirks and challenges, and, in
the process, we forged deep bonds.

The resident I got closest to was a man named Marvin. He
didn't talk and knew only a few signs, but we communicated
through my words and his gestures, headshakes, and grunts. He
liked to instigate a game by bringing his small hands up to my face
and, with a clap, pretending to slap me; for my part, I'd fall to the
ground in the most cartoonish fashion I could muster. I actually
accrued a lot of bruises that way, but it was worth it. After I'd fall,
he'd burst into the loudest laugh I'd ever heard. Putting up my fists
like a boxer and laughing, I'd tell Marvin that this wasn't over, but
two seconds later we'd be on to something else. He wanted a friend,
and though I wasn't supposed to be his friend, I was—and he was

mine. He'd often bring me a movie he wanted us to watch together, or a book to read, and we'd hang out like any other friend I had.

One evening Marvin grabbed my hand and brought me to his bedroom. He walked over to the bookshelf and grabbed a prayer book his brother had given him. As with any other book he wanted me to read from, he placed it in my hands. It was light, its edges shredded.

I cracked the book open and could see that it was well worn. Its pages, crinkled and torn, told me that this was a book that had known many days and many hands. I flipped through the pages and felt a knot in my stomach. *A prayer book?!* I thought. *Why did he have to bring me a prayer book?*

I tried to mask my cringe as I looked up at Marvin; his eyes, small and bright blue, searched my face in an attempt to understand my hesitation. I cleared my throat, rubbed my eyes, and asked him if he wanted me to read from it. He made a fist and slowly nodded it up and down, the sign for "yes." His head nodded, too, and he made a slight, crooked smile.

I turned to the "Lutheran Prayer for Courage," a page dog-eared for reference, and asked if he wanted me to read it. His hand again said "yes." I cleared my throat again and began to read aloud: "Lord God, you have called your servants to ventures of which we cannot see the ending, by paths as yet untrodden, through perils unknown. Give us faith to go out with good courage, not knowing where we go, but only that your hand is leading us and your love supporting us; through Jesus Christ our Lord. Amen."

I looked up. He was beaming. His arms, usually folded across his chest, had dropped down and relaxed, his hands clasped. I asked if he wanted to hear another, and he unclasped his hands, stood up, and gave me the tightest hug I've ever received, his face pressed against my blue flannel shirt. He didn't let go for at least a minute.

An unexpected feeling overtook me: relief. I had participated in a religious act with Marvin and I felt neither a strong desire to return to my Christian beliefs nor a disdain for his beliefs, as I so often had upon seeing any form of religious expression since I left Christianity.

In a way, reading the prayer felt like a conversion experience. It was profoundly different than simply "doing my job." It was entirely unlike previous times when I had read to Marvin. I could tell by the way he sat on the bed, instead of pacing the room as he usually did, that the prayer meant something very profound for him.

I realized that though I couldn't decipher *why* the prayer was so important to him, it was. It touched him in a profound way. And because I shared in this significant element of his life, our relationship was more honest and real. I could've found another staff member to do it, or I could've refused; it was well within my rights to say, "I'd rather not, Marvin." But I realized that a relationship that didn't account for this important piece of Marvin's life was an incomplete one. Though I couldn't fully comprehend the import of the prayer for him, sharing in it helped me understand him a bit more. Just as we had a communication barrier, this prayer was another difference between us. But like our different means of communicating, learning about our differences in this arena brought us closer together.

I said good night, walked back into the living room, and sat down on the sunken-in couch. *How much had I missed out on by refusing to entertain the religious lives of those I care about?* I immediately recalled my work with the Muslim community at Minneapolis's Brian Coyle Community Center through the Campus Kitchen at Augsburg College and how I had changed the subject any time something regarding religious beliefs came up; the condescending and dismissive way I had sometimes treated my religion professors and classmates at Augsburg; and the antireligious rhetoric that had prevented me from fully appreciating my study of liberation theology in El Salvador.

I spent that overnight shift cleaning the floors, the appliances, and the furniture, but I was focused on only one thing: even though I had spent my college years studying religious *texts*, I suddenly found myself wanting to learn more about the *lives* of religious *people*.

—⁓—

Living in Bemidji and being out of college afforded me the time to read books that weren't required reading, and after my prayer with Marvin, I started doing some research. Browsing Amazon.com, I stumbled upon Eboo Patel's *Acts of Faith: The Story of an American Muslim, The Struggle for the Soul of a Generation* and immediately recognized his name.

Eboo Patel had been the commencement speaker at Augsburg the semester before I graduated. He had laid out his vision for interfaith cooperation and explained how it might be realized on campuses like mine.

I, of course, hadn't gone. Looking back, I wish I had listened to my professor's advice and requested a ticket. I might have caught on to the idea of interfaith engagement sooner. But I hadn't been interested in hearing some hippy-dippy "religion as a force for good" message at that time, steeped as I was in my resentment toward religion.

I ordered the book and ripped the package open the moment it arrived. Reading Patel's story of growing up Muslim in America, I miraculously saw a lot of myself in it; all the more, his call for dialogue, for collaborative work, and for bridging diverse communities resonated deeply with my changed way of seeing the world. I already had the feeling, but he gave me the words.

I realized my approach to religion had been wrong and that I had been stunted by the pain of my negative religious experiences. By isolating myself from interreligious exchange, I missed opportunities to learn, to grow, and to collaborate around shared values. It struck me that throughout college, I had been doing interfaith work—with my classmates and professors, with the Muslim community in Minneapolis, with the people I met in El Salvador—but because I had checked my own values at the door and refused to engage on a deeper level, I had lost the chance to forge stronger connections and increase understanding.

It was clear that I needed to change my attitude toward religious people; it was holding me back in my relationships, in my work, and in my personal development—and it ran counter to the ethic of connection and service I'd cultivated all of my life. It was incomplete and inadequate—defined by caricature and critique instead of humility, honesty, and open-mindedness.

I wanted to learn from my mistakes and take concrete action to bridge the vast divide between religious communities and the nonreligious. The anger I felt after years of struggling with Christian theology and my sexual orientation transformed into something deeper, richer, and more complex: a combination of humility and empathy, a stance of conviction, curiosity, and compassion.

As much as I loved Bemidji and the people I had come to know and care for there, I knew that I had much more to learn if I was going to join Patel's efforts to make society more cooperative and less conflict-oriented. Deciding that I could learn a lot about bridging the divide between the religious and the secular by immersing myself once more in a religious institution, I looked at seminaries in Chicago, a city with more seminaries than any other on earth. I learned that if you enrolled in one, you could take courses at any of the others. That—along with the fact that Patel's organization,

Interfaith Youth Core, was based there—set my decision. It was time for this lifelong Minnesotan to leave the frigid North for the Windy City.

I promised to write letters to everyone and said my goodbyes, which was much harder than I could've imagined; when Marvin squeezed me and wouldn't let go, it took everything I had not to cry. I got in my car and drove home, where I sobbed until Kaitlin offered to take me to Burger King for a Whopper and a milkshake.

During my last week in Bemidji, the biggest blizzard of the season came through. It was May and we had already experienced spring weather, so this was totally unexpected. Kaitlin and I stayed inside that night while the sharp wind bellowed and the snow drowned the ground. I packed for Chicago as she worked on a painting, and the cat spent an hour trying to get behind the stove to a mysterious hole we dubbed "Narnia." The next morning, I woke up to more snow than I had ever seen, but the sun was brilliantly bright.

As I filled my final boxes, Okkervil River's "John Allyn Smith Sails"—a moving ode to deceased gay Minnesotan poet John Berryman—came on. It's one of my favorite songs by one of my favorite bands, for whom I have a tattoo on my right forearm, and I yelped along off-key to lyrics about a bright winter sun, moving on from a frozen town, and experiencing transformation. The song concluded as I crammed a Paul Bunyan t-shirt in the last box and taped it closed, the cardboard barely able to contain its contents.

I looked up at my window. The blinding snow had already begun to melt away, affording a clear view.

—⚭—

The transition from the rural north woods of Minnesota to Chicago couldn't have been more jarring and felt in line with my reshaped worldview. Though I had thought of Minneapolis as loud and diverse, Chicago was vibrant beyond anything I could've dreamed up. I spent my first few months before graduate school taking the subway to unfamiliar areas and getting to know the city. From the reinvented artists' haven/Mexican American enclave of Pilsen to the Indian hub of Rogers Park's Devon Avenue, I used my unlimited fare pass to ride the rails and discover a city perpetually in motion. My mom warned me that wandering a strange city without knowing what I was getting into spelled danger, but I could not resist: every corner I turned was more alive than the next.

She was right to worry. Early in my time in Chicago, I was exploring the city with several new friends when, out of nowhere, I heard a strident voice call, "Fags! Repent!"

Oh great—*those* words. Turning to meet the voice calling to me, I rolled my eyes as those funny, short sounds echoed and bounced toward me over hot, summer-baked pavement. The words were intended to hurt, but the insult fell flat. *I've heard much worse, and much more creative, fuckers*, I thought with a self-satisfied smile of superiority.

Still, I couldn't ignore them. My friends and I were in someone's crosshairs, singled out as needing salvation. With just two words, a divide was drawn between these strangers and my cohorts.

Did this really have to happen now? A couple of drinks in and feeling a bit defensive, I was newly twenty-one and just wanting to have fun. I wasn't sure I was really in the mood to navigate this verbal assault gracefully.

The battle cry had seemed to come from out of the ether. My friends and I were between bars, enjoying our evening, and ready for some spirited dancing. We weren't exactly a motley crew—sure, a good number of us were marked by tattoos, lightly adorned with piercings, regularly extinguishing cigarettes, and dressed in clothing that might raise a few Sunday-morning eyebrows, but we were an amicable bunch and my feeling is that most saw us as pretty harmless. Yet as we approached a queer bar one humid August night and prepared to pop, lock, and drop it, we were confronted by several men with Bibles in hand who accused us of maintaining an "alternative lifestyle"—a phrase that always makes me smirk— and offered our "offensive" appearance as evidence of this.

My friends were clearly caught off guard—after all, we were just there to have a good time—and responded defensively. In all fairness, I thought that some of what they had to say was not in the best taste. Slightly self-conscious about their responses to the Bible-carrying men, I thought to myself: *Well, politeness is not readily facilitated by beer and being the victim of a public ambush.*

Sensing escalation, I suggested my crew move inside, recognizing that the conversation was quickly becoming aggressively didactic, not thoughtfully dialogical. I would stay and talk with the men. My friends were happy to oblige—we had come to dance, not debate. A friend whispered in my ear as he passed by, "Are you going to be okay?"

I suddenly wasn't sure. This notion of employing empathy, of meeting people more than halfway when trying to transcend differences, was still pretty new to me. But I felt compelled to pursue a conversation.

Our exchange began with a reading from the Bible, which seemed less an attempt to open up the conversation with a graceful spirit than a blatant attempt to proselytize. I thanked them for sharing their holy book with me, and asked if they would like to explain why they had chosen to spend their Friday evening on this particular street corner. The missionaries informed me that they had recently given their lives over to Jesus Christ and had been commissioned by their minister to recruit other believers. They had heard that this part of Chicago was "heavily populated by homosexuals" and decided to come here to spread their message of reformation and repentance to a population they believed to be in need of it.

After hearing them out, I asked if I might be allowed to share my story with them. To my surprise, they nodded affirmatively. I told them of my years as a Christian and how immensely powerful they were for me—the love that I had experienced, the joy I had found in communion with other believers, and the inspiration that the story of Jesus Christ had provided me. But I also illuminated the darker side to those years: my struggles with recognizing my sexual orientation and wrestling to reconcile it with the teachings of the tradition, the shame I felt over who I was, and the weight of what felt like living a double life.

When I was finished, I noticed that a quiet had overtaken the group. Finally, one member spoke up. With a gruff tone and eyes fixed on the cracked concrete beneath his feet, he thanked me for sharing my story with him and told me that he had never actually known a "homosexual." He hadn't thought what it might be like to experience intolerance for being queer and compared it to the xenophobia and racism he had known as a Mexican American immigrant.

We engaged in open discourse for the next few hours with candor and respect, discussing discrimination and dancing and difference, beer and bigotry and basketball, religion and rap music and respect, fags and forgiveness and frijoles. Though we all remained relatively fixed in our convictions, we came to understand one another as fuller human beings instead of as mere caricatures of our sexualities or religious identities. I never saw them shout at gay people on that street corner again.

But, of course, not all conversations go as well as that one did. On another summer night just one month prior to this incident, my friend Joey and I waited for a train at 3 A.M. after a long night at a friend's birthday party. Though there were a few other people waiting around, the underground subway stop was desolate—a long, hollow tunnel, cavernous and damp. Joey wasn't feeling too well, so we sat on the ground and I ran my fingers across his back, scratching it while telling him funny anecdotes from my childhood to distract him from his stomachache.

This was the first time I had seen Joey, usually so brusque and proud, in a vulnerable state. I hadn't been in Chicago long, and he was the first real friend I'd made—rowdy and gruff, colorful and alive, and exactly what I had pictured when I first imagined a Chicagoan. But in the quiet of just-before-dawn, he let his guard down and opened up to me about his childhood. Away from all the family and friends I had ever known, this first moment of familial intimacy in our friendship was a respite.

"Hey fags, haven't you ever had good pussy before?!" I looked up to see a group of five guys looming over us, laughing and rubbing their hands together like we were kindling that would soon ignite a blaze.

We scrambled off the floor and stood to face them as they alternated between shouting offensive slurs and quoting the Bible at us, roaring with laughter, and striking intimidating poses. I was terrified, but I kept my cool and tried to come across as collected and unafraid. Joey returned their shouts at first but quickly fell silent in an attempt to keep himself from being ill and to keep them from hurting us.

This menacing game went on for what must have been thirty long minutes—they'd momentarily seem like they were less concerned with hurting us and more willing to see us as humans, but then the conversation would veer back into the obscene—until, finally, a train approached. I felt a sense of relief that I had kept them at bay and prevented the situation from escalating.

As the train roared toward us, its headlights filling the tunnel with light, the group swiftly, unexpectedly jumped us. Caught off guard, I was punched in the throat and shoved toward the tracks. Seeing that they had tried to push me onto the tracks right in front of the arriving train, Joey went red with rage and charged at the man responsible, who grabbed him by the neck and slammed him into the ground. I ran at them both, but Joey leapt up and pushed me into one of the train's now open doors—and, as he did, he took a blow to the back of the neck. Joey and I clawed our way onto the train; our attackers stayed behind on the platform to congratulate one another on a successful gay-bashing.

Heaving for breath, we collapsed onto the floor of the train. Moments later, a transit employee walked through our car, and we told him what had happened.

He kept on walking.

If this had happened just a year earlier, I would've been consumed by anger. Instead, I felt a deep sadness that threatened to overtake me. But suddenly—as suddenly as our attackers had jumped us—something inside of me shifted.

"Hey, do you want to get some breakfast?" I asked, turning to face Joey. "I could really go for something greasy, and I want to find a good spot to sit and talk for a long time so that we can figure out how we can make this fucked-up world just a little less fucked-up."

Tamping the blood running down his forehead with a scrap from his ripped t-shirt, Joey laughed and said, "Yeah, I could go for some food." And then, his face turned serious: "Chris—I'm a fighter. I can fend off those guys and others like them. But you—you're kinda fragile. You're going to have to figure out another way to take on guys like that."

"I know," I sighed, at risk of slipping back into self-pity. "I'm not sure where to start."

"I am," Joey replied with a typically mischievous grin. "With breakfast."

Many meals followed, and my circle of Chicago friends grew larger. Over gigantic chimichangas in a Logan Square restaurant that played telenovelas so loud that we felt as if we were characters inhabiting the shows, we dreamed up and debated ways to make the world a more tolerant place. But as encouraged as I felt in such moments, I could never forget the night Joey and I were attacked on the Chicago Red Line; how a growing crowd just watched in silence as we tried to fend off our attackers. Though I'd like to believe open dialogue can always overcome problematic conversations, the resolute remembrance of a bruised throat and a blow to the head reminded me that this is not true. As much as I'd like to think otherwise, I have learned that there are times where personal safety is a higher priority than respectful discourse.

Yet I will also always remember my night outside a gay bar, sharing stories with would-be proselytizers as bass-heavy music floated right on by me, carried away on a cool summer night's breeze. My friends were dancing just inside to a song I'd never know; I was enraptured by music much sweeter in the form of dialogue despite differences with new friends who were supposed to be enemies.

—m—

A few weeks later, fresh off the success of my positive interaction with those Christian proselytizers, I started seminary. Part of me couldn't believe I was actually going through with this—sure, I wanted to learn from the religious about how I might cross the interreligious and religious-secular chasms, but seriously? *Seminary?* I had winced at my fellow undergraduate religion majors who told me they were planning on theology school after college. But here I was, a seminary student.

I chose the master of arts in religion program at Meadville Lombard Theological School (MLTS) at the University of Chicago.

The Association of Chicago Theological Schools allowed me to take courses at any of the city's thirteen theological schools, and I was excited to take classes among Catholics, Protestants, Unitarian Universalists, Jews, Muslims, and others.

My first year of graduate school was difficult but rewarding. I was the first person in my immediate family to graduate from college, the first to pursue a master's, and the first to move away from Minnesota, and I missed being involved in the lives of my family members.

I was also the youngest student at my school by a significant margin, and I struggled to reconcile the religious terminology I heard with my secular outlook. The act of translating religious ideas into a secular framework helped me think outside the box, but at times it was just exhausting. Surrounded by religious thought, I found myself once again grappling with the questions that had brought me to Christianity in the first place, going so far as to declare in an essay: "I feel myself inching back toward a [non-anthropomorphic] God-concept." God seemed such an effective way to communicate ideas of justice and reconciliation, and I began to understand why so many used that framework when inviting people to act in love and empathy.

But I ultimately stuck with my conclusion that, for me and many others, theism doesn't make sense. A professor once said to me: "When I talk about God, I mean love and justice and reconciliation, not a man in the sky. You talk about love and justice and reconciliation—why can't you just call that God?" My reply was short and firm: "Why *must* you call that God? Why not just call it what it is: love and justice and reconciliation?" These debates raged on with no neat and tidy consensus reached; however, we both learned a lot from one another.

Yet, as in my undergraduate years, what I learned outside the classroom enriched me the most during my graduate-school years.

I was fortunate to enter MLTS in the pilot year of their Community Partnership Program and was placed at Woodlawn Youth Solutions (WYS), a partnership of the Brickyard Community Garden and Christ Way Missionary Baptist Church.

Missionary? Baptist? Church? I thought. *Oh boy. Let's see how this works.*

It was one thing to read *Acts of Faith* and think, *Yeah! That whole interfaith social action thing sounds great!* But actually taking that step into the unknown was, while exciting, terribly daunting.

Located in one of Chicago's most crime-ridden neighborhoods, where over half of the households received some form of public aid, WYS offered the youth of Woodlawn an alternative to the neighborhood's rampant violence: a safe space in which homework was done before anything else, activities were collaborative and educational, and children less than half my height schooled me in basketball.

But it was far from idyllic. One day, several children ran up to me and said, "Chris, guess what happened at school today?"

I couldn't read their expressions; their faces were flushed. I wondered: Did they hear a speaker? Did they go on a field trip?

"There was a chalk outline outside the school! That means someone got shot there today."

My stomach dropped. I wanted to grab those kids and give them the biggest hug I could muster, but I knew they would look at me like I was suddenly possessed. News like this was not uncommon for them, and it underscored why this program was so needed. WYS was a haven from the violence of their neighborhood. It was a space where education was prioritized and kids were encouraged to pursue diverse interests. It was a resource for the South Side's burgeoning community garden movement. And it was a church.

I thought back to the violence I had experienced on the Red Line one day within months of moving to Chicago and of the violence these kids lived with every day. These incidents felt connected, like two strands in a systemic social web. Our struggle against violence was a shared one.

The WYS programming was diverse, focusing on education and community. In late October of 2008, as a historic presidential election was building to its monumental conclusion, we had an election event at a senior center a few blocks away. The kids made cookies, which we brought to the residents. We asked the seniors if they were voting, and they shared with the WYS youth why they thought voting was important. One week later, we held another election event: a party that Meadville Lombard offered to host. The kids decorated cookies with quotes on the importance of voting and gave them to people walking around the neighborhood. Because MLTS was in Barack Obama's neighborhood, one of two national C-SPAN studio buses was in the area and invited our group inside for a tour and an interview. The WYS youth, bursting with excitement and self-confidence, sang a song they invented on the spot for the C-SPAN cameras: "Have a cookie and a quote; it only matters if you vote!"

WYS was created to help kids focus on their futures, but they were still kids. During homework time, they would always try to find a way to put off getting their work done by talking to me. I'd usually humor them with a quick exchange and then encourage them to finish their work, but every once in a while someone would say something that would ensnare me. Once, a young man with short hair and a large orange shirt called me "Chris Breezy." When I asked him what it meant, he said it was his way of comparing me to the pop singer Chris Brown, who'd recently been arrested for domestic abuse. When I suggested that the comparison was inappropriate, all of the kids chimed in that I should be flattered because Brown was "cool and has fly style like you do!"

My "style"—my clothing and body modifications (especially my stretched earlobes)—were a hot topic of conversation among the WYS youth, particularly among those who were trying to avoid doing their homework. "Whoa, I can see through your ears!" they'd shout, intrigued and slightly disturbed. One day, I forgot to wear a long-sleeved shirt, which left my tattooed arms exposed. Several of the kids said they thought my tattoos were drawings, until one precocious young woman with a sparkly t-shirt named Larissa told them, "I think it's 'cause his skin is so light, that's why they look fake."

I usually managed to wrap up these conversations fairly quickly so the kids could focus on their homework, but one day, a young man named Michael posed a question that I was completely unable to deflect.

It was a simple question: "Chris, why do you come here?"

"What do you mean?"

"I mean, why do you come here?" he repeated, setting down his pencil and looking me squarely in the face. "You don't have to, right? You ain't getting paid, so why you here? For school?"

"Well, I'm here because I like working with you guys," I began, pulling out the empty chair next to him and sitting down. I noticed that his shoelaces were untied. "It's enjoyable for me. But you're right that I'm also here as a part of a program at my school."

"What's your major?" he asked, and I realized how little I'd actually shared about my life with the kids at WYS.

"Well, I study religion. I'm doing my master's, which is something you can do after you finish college if you want to do more school."

"You study religion?" He paused and I couldn't read his expression. "Is you going to be a minister?"

"No, I'm not going to be a minister," I said, stifling a laugh. "I'm not actually religious. But I do study religion."

"All religions?" he gasped with excitement, his words tumbling one over another. "No way, we just studied world religions in school!"

"Yes, all religions," I affirmed. "What religions did you study?"

"Christianity, Jewish, Islam," he said slowly. "Buddhism . . . Hindu-nism?"

"Hinduism?" I asked, and he nodded. "Wow, that's great!" I continued, impressed that he was already learning about religion at school. "Did you learn anything interesting?"

"Oh yeah, lots of stuff," he said, looking up at the ceiling. "But I can't believe you study religion; that really surprises me, man."

"It does? Why does it surprise you?"

"I don't know—I don't really see you studying religions." Michael smiled. "I just don't get that vibe."

I wasn't surprised; his question was one I'd fielded from friends and even from some of my fellow seminarians. "Why do *you* study religion?" I was still answering it myself.

"So, what vibe do you get?" I asked, curious.

"I dunno," he paused. "Not that one, though. But that's cool, man."

"Thank you, Michael," I responded. "I study religion because lots of people are religious, and there are a lot of different religions, and everyone practices them differently. I think it's important to know what other people believe, and how that affects the kinds of decisions they make."

"Oh! That's cool," he said, sitting up straight. "My neighbor's a Muslim, and I don't know very much about that. Maybe I should ask him to tell me about it sometime," he said, grinning proudly.

"That's not a bad idea, Michael," I said. "You probably should!" But immediately after saying this, I got nervous; would his parents be mad? What if Michael heard more about Islam and decided he wanted to become a Muslim? The idea that interfaith dialogue puts people—especially children—at risk of losing or changing their faith is a contentious issue in many communities, even though my colleagues and I haven't yet encountered anyone who has experienced such a change (in fact, the opposite is often true).

Still, deep and frank conversations with people with different religious or nonreligious beliefs often *do* feel quite risky, and I wondered: Was I putting the kids at risk with my ideas? Was I putting myself at risk?

Yet sitting there in a green plastic chair five sizes too small for my six foot, four inch frame, I knew that it was a risk worth taking. I had played it safe for too long and I was tired of skirting around important pieces of identity—mine and those of the people I encountered.

A few weeks later, I asked Michael if he had talked to his Muslim neighbor. He told me that he'd asked his mother about it, and they invited their neighbor over for dinner.

"My mom said Jesus was friends with everybody so we should be too," Michael said with excitement, pleased to report that he had followed through on his bright idea. "I asked him about Muslims and he was really smart and I don't think we're even all that different in the end because we like a lot of the same things. Plus, he brought over mac and cheese that he made himself and it was the best ever!"

After a year exploring Chicago, I had seen the difference between pockets of diversity coexisting peacefully and the possibility that comes from real, honest, and even somewhat risky engagement. As my first year of seminary came to a close, I recalled my other motivation behind looking at Chicago for seminary and remembered that it hadn't just been because it was the closest sprawling metropolis to Minneapolis. Reading Eboo Patel's *Acts of Faith* had inspired me to do this work, and his organization, Interfaith Youth Core (IFYC), was headquartered there.

Thinking back to my night outside that gay bar, I knew that Michael, his Christian mother, and his Muslim neighbor represented a new kind of interchange. But I still didn't know how to make it into something more than a shared meal of macaroni and cheese.

As summer approached, I knew I had to take this idea to the next level somehow. And then an e-mail from IFYC landed in my inbox.

—⚍—

As I sat on a barely upholstered plastic seat on a Blue Line train, one foot propped up on the seat beside me, I ran my thumb over the glossy dial of my MP3 player and selected a song. Wilco's "Theologians" coursed through the wires of my headphones and blared into my ears, and I nodded as Jeff Tweedy declared in the opening lines that theologians were ignorant about his soul.

As I listened, I wondered how an intentionally interfaith group would function. Would they have some big surface-level lovefest? Or deeper, harder conversations? The image of a "Kumbaya" drum circle popped into my mind, and I shuddered just a little.

I was headed to the Greektown offices of Interfaith Youth Core for my first day as an intern. I was looking forward to meeting everyone, but I was admittedly most excited to meet its founder and president Eboo Patel. In the year that had passed since I had read his book, he had been named to President Obama's Advisory Council on Faith-Based and Neighborhood Partnerships and had received countless awards and accolades. And though my excitement to meet him had guided me to IFYC, the first thing I noticed upon walking into his office was—coincidentally—a colossal Wilco poster on his wall.

The Wilco poster gave me a sense of commonality with Eboo, but there were also several symbols of his Muslim faith, from a prominently displayed Quran to a framed "Bisma'llah" illustration. Here I was, in the presence of a deeply religious man, trying to explain why I thought interfaith work mattered—and suddenly I started to feel unsure of what role I could play in the movement. Sure, we both liked Wilco, but was that enough to bring together a Muslim and an atheist?

I recalled what my secular friends had said before I moved to Chicago. "I just don't understand what is drawing you to religion," they'd sigh, adding a Jeff Tweedy-esque comment about my ambitions: "You know, I just don't *get* religious people. And they certainly don't get me."

A few months before I stood in Eboo's office for the first time, I had gathered together a group of my new Chicago friends to celebrate my birthday. Before people got some drinks in them and religious differences no longer seemed to matter, half of my friends were standing on one side of the room and half were on the other. You could practically draw a chalk line down the middle of the room, and if that line had a name, it would be what Eboo calls "the faith divide." Anyone who looked even remotely religious—a distinction I didn't totally understand that seemed abundantly clear to others, though I suspect it had something to do with style of dress—was given a suspicious sideways glance by my nonreligious friends as they went outside for their continual cigarette breaks. From inside the party, I heard them hiss: "What are *they* doing here? Did he really have to invite his Jesus-y friends? Some of them aren't even drinking!"

It's not like I don't understand the secular apprehension about religious people. Once you've been burned, you're less likely to set foot in the kitchen. But here I was in that kitchen again—an atheist seminary student, standing in the office of a national faith leader—and the heat was getting to me. Suddenly I thought of Moses in the Book of Exodus asking God, "Who am I that I should go to Pharaoh and bring the Israelites out of Egypt?" My mission was not so immense, of course, but I still wondered: *Was I capable of working to bridge the divide between different religions? And what about the chasm between the religious and the secular?*

The doubt and confusion that first emerged in Eboo's office didn't subside right away—for my first few months at IFYC, I was plagued by both. I initially wondered if there was a place for me as a nonreligious person in the interfaith movement, but after building relationships with my colleagues and with student leaders, I began to see that atheists and agnostics are more than just welcome in the interfaith movement: our role is important.

Whether it was my supervisor Cassie, who invited me to see her perform at her church and who, knowing I might be a little uncomfortable in such a setting, played Sufjan Stevens as the service's prelude to make me feel at home, or Mary Ellen, another atheist and Humanist who understood my struggle to situate myself in this movement, who would take me to get coffee and offer advice and crack jokes, I was roundly welcomed and made to feel like I was a critical part of the equation.

My biggest concern about interfaith work—that it was only sustainable when everyone "played nice" and checked their real opinions at the door—was regularly disproved. After a daylong staff meeting in my fourth month on the job, Amber, a deeply committed Christian staff member who was the internship coordinator, offered to give me a ride to the subway as it was raining. She and I had become good friends as we worked together, and we'd gotten to a point where we could speak candidly and openly. After some small talk, Amber and I started talking about her faith.

"Can I be honest with you, Chris?" she asked, her eyes focused on the road, piercing past her windshield wipers.

"Of course," I responded, turning to look at her.

She pushed several strands of striking blonde hair behind her right ear. "You know I respect what you do, and what you're all about," she said cautiously.

I laughed before I could stop myself and said, again, "Of course!"

"But, if I can tell you the truth, I do worry about your salvation sometimes," she said, momentarily taking her eyes off the road to look at me. "You must know that I do, right?" She was smiling optimistically, a flash of trepidation in the greens of her eyes.

"Well, I mean, yeah," I said with a chuckle, adjusting the seat belt that had ridden up to my neck. "You're a Christian, so it doesn't exactly surprise me."

"Well, sometimes I think about how you used to be a Christian, and it honestly makes me sad that you aren't anymore. Again, you know, I respect what you're doing so much," she said, and I was warmed by her concern and protectiveness. "In fact, I struggle with my feelings about your salvation, because the truth is that I don't really *want* you to stop what you're doing. Your perspective is important to me and for our work together, and I feel like I'd lose out on something if you became a Christian again. So it's a tension I have to live with, but I wanted to be honest with you about it." We came to a red light and she turned to face me again.

"Amber," I started. "Thank you. I mean, you could've kept that to yourself, but I'm glad you didn't. And you must know that I, as an atheist, think your beliefs are probably wrong, too."

"Of course," she said, turning off the car radio. "It's kind of funny to think about just how different our worldviews are, but how similar our views are, right?"

"Totally," I laughed. "Think about it: a committed Christian and an avowed atheist; a traditional blonde 'southern belle' and a tattooed queer. Working together to build a movement. Around religion. It kind of sounds like a punch line, doesn't it?"

It did then, but it doesn't anymore. Now it sounds like exactly what our world needs—people of all different stripes and convictions coming together to deal with things that matter, announcing our differences without fear, enthusiastically embracing our commonalities, and intentionally seeking out points of mutuality and understanding in the face of vastly different metaphysical commitments. The environment that IFYC worked to create has profoundly impacted my vision for a society in which people engage across lines of religious and nonreligious identity to improve the world through service, and it is because of my relationships with people like Amber that I feel equipped to work toward that vision.

My work was often "behind-the-scenes" stuff—planning IFYC's biannual conference, developing content for trainings, sending e-mails, and creating elaborate Excel spreadsheets—but even there, the interactions were rich. Everyone at IFYC knew we were building something larger than a spreadsheet, larger than ourselves, and larger than our differences.

The conversations that grew out of this work were often startling in their impact. Working on promotion for the biannual conference, a fellow intern named Sayira and I got to talking to dull the pain of repetitive e-mailing. She told me about a man she had a crush on, and as we glanced up from our computer screens every other minute, we swapped several dating stories.

After a few of these accounts, Sayira turned away from her computer screen and offered a confession: "I've never really met a gay person before," she said, "besides the ones I've kicked and punched."

She was referring to the LGBTQ people at her karate dojo, and I pointed out the unintentional humor in what she had said. We both laughed for a good fifteen minutes.

"But like I was saying, I've never really talked to them before. So, can I ask?" she continued, regaining her composure. "What do you look for in men?"

To her, she explained, faith was a priority when seeking a suitor. The guy she was interested in was a Christian, and though it was not her religion, she was relieved that he believed. I told her that there are a lot of things that attract me to a person, but that I'm often drawn to compassion, empathy, creativity, and a desire to be a better person and build a better society. She scooted her chair across the room with a smile and replied that what appealed to her about her interest's religiosity was that he had a value system. I agreed that principles are critical, and we kept talking as we e-mailed, uncovering a previously unknown swath of common ground as the sun set outside our office window.

Before that afternoon, we didn't think we had much in common, but by sharing our experiences, another unlikely duo—a secular queer and a Muslim woman—uncovered a shared respect for ethics. That day we each discovered ourselves in the other's story, and we were both transformed. As we sent e-mails that would lead to a conference full of expansive interfaith dialogue and action for others, our own worlds became just a little bit larger.

Eboo wrote in *Acts of Faith* that "when thousands of people discover that their story is also someone else's story, they have the chance to write a new story together."[1] The moment I shared my story as an atheist, others felt more comfortable sharing their own—whether those stories were about religion, identity, or social change. As Christian author William White once said, "The most natural response to one story is another story."[2]

As I worked with more and more communities around interfaith issues, it became apparent that, in a culture dominated by religious politics and conflict, sharing experiences of cooperation across lines of difference was essential, and that there was a hunger for doing so. As I heard countless stories of religious identity—how interfaith proponents were enriched and nurtured by their own traditions and values—I started to realize that nonreligious accounts were often missing from the conversation. *If so many different people can come together around diverse religious stories,* I thought, *certainly we secular folks have our own to share. If only we would step up, I know one religious man with a Wilco poster on his office wall who is more than happy to listen.*

I turned twenty-three while working with IFYC, and to celebrate I invited people from every sector of my life to join me: interfaith activists, queer hipster DJs, seminarians, and friends from high school. Gathered in a dim and dusty dive bar, my Chicago friends came together and my various worlds intermingled. Thinking back to the awkward beginning of my birthday celebration just one year before, I wondered whether my friends would get along. But there was no divide this time: everyone gathered around a group of six tables pushed together, with Tom Waits's "Chocolate Jesus" on the jukebox, and we all shared in one another's stories of religious and secular identity, social change, and the diverse issues that mattered most to us. And then, after hours of first-rate conversation, we stood up and danced.

As I looked around at my very own "beloved community" of friends and co-workers, Muslims and Jews, filmmakers and ministers, atheists and queers, I thought of Cassie's church and Sayira's mosque, and I began to wonder: *What could a community of atheists look like?*

7

In Search of
the Secular Soul

We are healthy only to the extent that our ideas are humane.

—Kurt Vonnegut, *Breakfast of Champions*

It's funny that, after searching so long for an identity that affirmed my naturalistic worldview and compassionate ambitions, I finally found Secular Humanism because of a Muslim.

After years of evading discussions about the reality of other people's religious identities, I had faltered when discerning how to identify myself. When I realized how much of an impediment my attitude toward the religious was in my personal development, I still wasn't sure what to call myself. I used "atheist," "agnostic," "nonreligious," and "secular" interchangeably, but none of them really felt right; while each was accurate, they all seemed a bit inadequate—more like descriptors than identities. None encapsulated how I saw the world; none felt like an affirmation of the values I held. So I just went about doing interfaith work without an affiliation, content to create opportunities for people of varying worldviews to engage with one another constructively. Still, I wasn't completely sure how to articulate my own perspective.

But through the process of doing interfaith work—through building relationships of understanding and cooperation with religious people—that began to change. Inspired by others' commitments to their varying worldviews, I began to more deeply consider my own. While working at IFYC, Eboo introduced me to Greg Epstein's *Good Without God* and the works of other contemporary Humanists. I began to devour Humanist literature; from Confucius, Epicurus, and Renaissance Humanism up to more recent Humanist thinkers like Robert G. Ingersoll and Paul Kurtz. I read the various editions of the Humanist Manifestos and jumped up excitedly to repeat them aloud: "Humanism is a progressive philosophy of life that, without supernaturalism, affirms our ability and responsibility to lead ethical lives of personal fulfillment that aspire to the greater good of humanity."[1] This was what I believed—particularly its emphasis on taking personal responsibility for the greater good of all—but another person had written it down.

Inspired by what I'd read, I decided to act. Along with a group of other atheist friends, my friend Erik and I started up a group we called the Secular Humanist Alliance of Chicago, to construct an egalitarian community of like-minded individuals. We planned service projects, hosted dialogue events with members of Chicago's Muslim community, and wrote blog posts. But more than anything else, we were a community.

Encouraged by the books I read and the subsequent conversations I had with these friends, I started see my Humanism as not just something I thought about, but something I needed to act upon. This positive orientation of my Humanism allowed me to frame the world through a constructive, optimistic lens, and it became an expression of my greatest ambitions—one that sought out and celebrated the good in everyone, and encouraged me to act with love and compassion whenever possible, seeking to understand instead of dismiss.

For the first time in as long as I could remember, I felt invested in a positive and deeply personal identity that pretty accurately mapped onto my own convictions. And, as is the case whenever I'm excited about something, I couldn't shut up about it.

—∿—

While I was working at IFYC, Eboo invited me to submit a guest piece for his Washington Post *On Faith* column. At the time, I was beginning to recognize that organized atheism often talked about religion in ways that created more division instead of less—and largely talked about itself by defining what it wasn't at the expense of articulating Humanist values. As an atheist I was frustrated by what I saw as a lack of interest from my fellow atheists in respectfully engaging religious identities and how the confrontation of religious beliefs seemed to trump the pursuits of self-awareness or bettering the conditions of life for others. So I sat down and wrote about it.

After my submission was posted, I started getting some unexpected feedback. "This is exactly what I think, but I didn't know anyone else agreed with me," wrote one reader. "Thank you for saying something our community really needs to hear," wrote another. I hadn't really thought about the fact that there were probably many others who felt the same way I did, and I felt compelled to continue the conversation somehow. I talked to Erik, who managed a queer music blog, and he suggested I create a blog of my own to continue sorting through this issue.

I started *NonProphet Status* and suddenly became a part of a larger conversation on the intersection of religion and atheism. I began to hear from countless others who said that they too did not believe in God but didn't feel compelled to define themselves in opposition to the religious. The blog quickly gained traction in interfaith and atheist circles, and soon I was being asked to speak at conferences, receiving invitations to write in more prominent venues, and watching my blog views grow from week to week. I, a young student with a small but growing vision for respectful engagement across lines of secular and religious identity, suddenly had a platform.

I did not think that productive religious-nonreligious cooperation was a new idea, but many people I met indicated that they had never heard anyone else articulate it. I invited those who also perceived a need for atheists to practice and promote constructive dialogue with the religious to share in the platform I'd been fortunate enough to acquire. I had plenty to say, but I met many other people who did, too, and I wanted to help make their voices heard. I felt so strongly about this that I eventually joined forces with the Journal of Inter-Religious Dialogue (JIRD) and the Council for a Parliament of the World's Religions (CPWR) to found a website intended to lift up emerging ethical voices in dialogue. I suggested we name it *State of Formation* because I felt I had benefited from the opportunity to develop my voice in a public dialogue with others and wanted to work with my colleagues at JIRD and CPWR to create a space where others could do the same. Reading the work of other individuals grappling with similar issues helped me to refine my own perspective.

As I started to write about this work for a broader audience and speak with others in communities across the country who have had unique challenges and successes in bridging the gap between the religious and the nonreligious, I began to understand that my desire to do interfaith work was an outgrowth of my Humanistic principles. The opportunities I had to bring religious and nonreligious people together for dialogue and collaborations began to increase, and I found it harder and harder to think that this work could be a hobby or something I just did in my free time. Lying in my bed after one of a growing number of workshops I facilitated, I felt immense gratitude for the people in my life—for my community. *This is Humanism,* I thought, *and it is far better than anything I could ever dream up.*

Waking up the next morning, I knew what I wanted to do with my life. I wanted to help organize nonreligious communities that would not only provide a safe space for the nonreligious but would also value reaching out to those with different beliefs in an attempt to understand and empathize, not bulldoze or mock them.

After years of feeling like a person on the margins of cohesive communities, I'd found a confidence in my own beliefs as an atheist and a Humanist that enabled me to adopt an inquiring and empathic approach to difference. I'd met enough people in the atheist and Humanist movements who felt the same way, and I wanted to work with them to build up institutions and spaces for the nonreligious that provided resources for people to live flourishing lives of fulfillment alongside and with the religious.

After a year and a half working at Interfaith Youth Core, I made the difficult decision to leave the organization. I was far from finished with interfaith work, but I had honed in on what I wanted to do: work on interfaith cooperation from a position in the Humanist community. I drew encouragement from a commencement address delivered in 1974 by self-identified Humanist Kurt Vonnegut. In this speech, he said: "What should young people do with their lives today? Many things, obviously. But the most daring thing is to create stable communities in which the terrible disease of loneliness can be cured."[2]

Around the time I realized that I wanted to work to help build a Humanist community, I got a call from an unknown number. It was Greg Epstein, the Humanist chaplain at Harvard University and author of *Good Without God,* whom I'd met through my work at IFYC.

A few months later, I moved out East to create a pilot interfaith community service program for the Humanist Chaplaincy at Harvard.

—ᴍ—

I started at the Humanist Chaplaincy at Harvard two years after my experience working with Christ Way Missionary Baptist Church on the South Side of Chicago. I cherished the experiences I had in that community and often recalled what I'd learned there when I worked on chaplaincy programs—but when I tried to talk to some fellow atheists about those experiences, many were shocked and asked how I could work in an environment in which they assumed people would despise me for being gay and an atheist. Some of them even castigated me for "supporting oppression" by working in a church. I was baffled.

Early on in my time with the chaplaincy I got an e-mail from my friend Toby, who was working for an organization called SOUL (Southsiders Organizing for Unity and Liberation), a largely (but not exclusively) church-based community organization that works in the South Side and southern suburbs of Chicago, fighting for the interests of a hugely neglected region. He knew of my work in the atheist movement and wanted to let me know that the Freedom from Religion Foundation was running a series of bus ads in the neighborhood in which I used to work. One, which he had only seen run on bus routes on the South Side, featured a picture of Butterfly McQueen, of *Gone with the Wind* fame, along with a quote from her: "As my ancestors are free from slavery, I am free from the slavery of religion."

We both agreed that the quote itself was not inherently problematic—leaving religion behind can be a truly liberating experience for many people, as it was for McQueen. We also agreed that the idea that an advertisement might have been designed to target Chicago's large black population wasn't necessarily inappropriate; many black atheists I've spoken with have told me that they feel especially isolated, so a message telling them they aren't alone would be a good thing.

The issue we both had with the ad is that the legacy of real, *literal* slavery still looms large on the South Side. As Toby wrote:

> [The legacy of slavery] lingers in the air, thick and ugly; it sucks out economic and social vitality, leaving behind vacant lots and broken homes, misery and anxiety. Although slavery has been abolished on paper, in reality its spirit persists in innumerable afterimages. Through the metaphor of religion-as-slavery, the FFRF leapfrogs over all of these: the lack of access to decent (or any) jobs, the third of black men who will be incarcerated in their lifetime, the one-in-ten black families who will be evicted every year. (These trends are getting worse, not better.) Oh, but never mind these: apparently religion is the one big problem remaining in the lives of black people, the one thing they need to get over in order to be truly free.

Regardless of what some people think about the truth of religious claims, and regardless of what people think of the good and bad done by religious institutions, there is one very good reason for why SOUL does the bulk of its organizing work in churches, and why you interned at one. It's the same reason churches were so essential to organizing and funding the Civil Rights Movement. Saul Alinsky, one of the key figures in the history of community organizing, said that there are two forms of power: organized money and organized people. In our increasingly fractured society, there are fewer and fewer institutions where you can organize enough people to counter the weight of all the organized money that's out there nowadays. And one of those institutions—the only one on the Southside, really—is the church.

Based on my year of working out of a church on Chicago's South Side, I knew he was right—religious organizations, especially churches and mosques, are the lifeblood of that community. And given my familiarity with the devastating socioeconomic conditions of that region, I was flabbergasted that the financial resources dedicated by this atheist organization to fund a project intended to benefit the residents of the South Side were put toward, of all things, a bus ad that probably did little to directly benefit anyone living there. Was there really no better way to spend that money?

The disheartening news about the bus ads was just one of many reasons that I began to question the priorities of the atheist movement. It seemed to me that the majority of the movement's resources was being poured into aggressive antireligious campaigns.

The strong antireligious ethos of the movement made it difficult for me to carry over the work I was doing in the interfaith movement into the atheist movement. Though I had faced challenges in interfaith contexts, those I encountered in the atheist movement were very different, and I struggled to acclimate to a new environment.

Atheism itself is hardly new, but the dizzying rise of an organized movement in the United States is relatively recent. In 2006, *Wired* magazine dubbed the popular atheistic movement initiated by authors Richard Dawkins, Christopher Hitchens, Sam Harris, and Daniel Dennett as "New Atheism." The movement, sometimes said to have been a reaction to the terrorist attacks against the United States on September 11, 2001 (popular atheist blogger Greta Christina has called 9/11 the atheist Stonewall), was catalyzed by a slew of books and subsequent media coverage.[3]

It is clear that the percentage of the population that identifies as religiously unaffiliated is growing—according to the 2008 American Religious Identification Survey, 15 percent of Americans report having no religion and 22 percent of Americans ages eighteen to twenty-nine fall into this category—but only about 2 percent of Americans describe themselves with labels such as atheist, agnostic, Humanist, and less widely recognized identifiers like "freethinker" or "bright."[4] So, though atheism's visibility has increased in recent years, the number of self-identified atheist Americans remains a fraction of the nonreligious.

That said, the atheist movement itself has seen incredible growth as an organized force. The Secular Student Alliance, a vital organization that coordinates college and university groups for atheists, agnostics, and the nonreligious, shows rapid growth of nontheistic groups, particularly over the last five years: the number of affiliated groups grew from 50 in 2006 to over 260 in 2011. In the wake of the rise of New Atheism, more and more atheists have begun to organize.

As I explored the rise of atheism, I discovered that most self-declared atheists have little in common, save one thing: we do not believe in God. But I also saw that the dominant narrative of the atheist movement was fueled by people positioning themselves in stark opposition to religion and the religious—the so-called New Atheists who have managed to monopolize the public discourse on atheism. They have succeeded in making atheism more publicly known, but at what cost? Atheist identity remains hugely unpopular, with polls showing we are the least electable group in America, behind gay people and African Americans.[5]

That nontheist identity is being popularly defined as explicitly nonreligious isn't itself problematic; an integral aspect of atheist identity is understandably rooted in the idea that we are *not* religious. But in recent years the New Atheists have taken this a step further, marking atheism as being uniformly equivalent to antithe-ism. When the majority of prominent atheist-identified thought leaders name "the end of faith" as one of the movement's top pri-orities, the idea of participating in organized interfaith efforts can seem contradictory.[6]

This was intimately clear to me as I started to dedicate a good deal of time to meeting and speaking with other atheists at conferences and events. As I took the idea of interfaith coopera-tion into the organized atheist movement, I met many wonder-ful people dedicated to the same ideals as I was and learned a lot about others' experiences of being in a small minority. But I was also quickly taken aback by the amount of antireligious rhetoric I heard—and the degree of negativity directed at me for questioning it. For the most part, the antireligious claims I encountered weren't considered critiques of theology, which I've often relished in both academic and interpersonal contexts; they were based in a willful ignorance of what it actually means to be religious and of the way religious lives are lived, and turned religious people into a cheaply mocked caricature.

My first atheist conference, an American Atheists gathering in New Jersey, was packed full of blasphemy sessions and speeches comparing religion to sexually transmitted diseases. It was, for me, a nightmare. Witnessing the sheer vitriol some expressed toward the religious, I actually cried—hot, angry tears. I called friends of mine back home—atheists, no less—and recalled what I'd seen. They were shocked and appalled. One friend said to me: "You see, this is why I don't want to call myself an atheist." I returned to my work in an interfaith context and was relieved to be surrounded by people dedicated to advancing human rights and understanding, not dehumanizing those with different metaphysical beliefs.

The atheist movement is doing something very wrong when a sizable number of the atheists I meet in my day-to-day life want nothing whatsoever to do with it. But I started actively participating—and have stuck with the movement even when I wanted to walk away—because I believe there is truly invaluable work happening there. I have met more people than I can count who are boldly creating safe spaces for atheists to find support and positively impact the world, and I am inspired by their activism; but I remain deeply concerned by the dehumanizing antireligious ethos overtaking a movement that essentially speaks for me and others who actively claim that they do not believe in any gods.

For example: one of my favorite aspects of my job is that I get to plan and lead a group of Harvard Humanist graduate students on a spring-break service trip. The first year I was on staff at the chaplaincy, I worked with our students to plan a trip to South Dakota to work with at-risk youth from the Cheyenne River Reservation. It was an incredible week; not only because of the work we were able to do but also because of the tight bond we formed as a group. While there, I had some illuminating conversations with several students from the University of Iowa who were also on site to volunteer. They too were atheists but declined to call themselves that or get involved in organized atheism precisely because they saw it as divisive, mean-spirited, and in contradiction with their personal values. After meeting and working with our group, they began to ask us how they could get involved in or start up a Humanist community but acknowledged they wouldn't have done so before. And they're far from the only people I've met who feel that way; in fact, I know more atheists and agnostics who decline to identify with or participate in the atheist movement because of their concerns about organized atheism than I can recount.

I believe that broadening the aims of the atheist movement to be more affirming and less antagonistic will mean that it will have more to offer people—that it will contribute something positive to their lives—and I believe that if the movement shifts in that direction, it can and will bring in folks who currently don't feel welcome.

I'd like to see our community find ways to not only be open to the religiosity of our friends and loved ones so that we do not miss opportunities to learn by listening, but I also hope that we will focus less on what sets us apart and more on articulating our positive values. Where atheism is lacking, religion will continue to thrive.

—⁓—

The problem here isn't just that the atheist movement isn't providing adequate resources for all of the nonreligious. It's also that across-the-board antireligious attitudes are making it more difficult for us to build necessary alliances.

When I meet a Christian woman at the airport and the subject of my work comes up, I hasten to reassure her that I'm not bent on destroying her faith after her face turns sour at the word "atheist." When I facilitate an interfaith dialogue with the hope that it will lead to a generation of young people who do not see religious diversity as a cause for division, I worry that the revelation that I do not believe in God myself may prove a stumbling block because all they claim to hear coming from the atheist camp is "your beliefs are so stupid to me that I will go out of my way to ensure that you know it." And I'm tired of turning red when friends of mine ask if I've seen the episode of *The Daily Show* where host Jon Stewart eviscerates the American Atheists' latest headline-grabbing stunt by highlighting a statement by the organization's president, Dave Silverman, regarding a piece of rubble in the shape of a cross placed in the World Trade Center memorial museum: "The WTC cross has become a Christian icon. It has been blessed by so-called holy men and presented as a reminder that their god, who couldn't be bothered to stop the Muslim terrorists or prevent

3,000 people from being killed in his name, cared only enough to bestow upon us some rubble that resembles a cross." Speaking as if he were Silverman, Stewart added to Silverman's inflammatory remarks: "As President of the American Atheists organization, I promise to make sure that everyone, even those that are indifferent to our cause, will fucking hate us." It's no wonder so many do.

Indiscriminate attacks on "religion," as if it were a single note instead of a complex chord, are a very real problem because they obscure Humanism's larger aims—making the world a better, more rational place—with a distracting, destructive, and alienating narrative that doesn't account for differences in belief and practice. Such behavior fundamentally limits who our movement appeals to and distracts us from focusing on cultivating our own uniquely secular ethics.

In the introduction to his book *I Don't Believe in Atheists*, Chris Hedges writes:

> I paid little attention, until these two public debates, to the positions of "New Atheist" thinkers, who sometimes are called, or call themselves, "new atheists." After all, there is nothing intrinsically moral about being a believer or a non-believer. There are many people of great moral probity and courage who seek meaning outside of formal religious structures, who reject religious language and religious ritual and define themselves as atheists. There are also many religious figures that in the name of one god or another sanctify intolerance, repression and violence.
>
> The agenda of the new atheists, however, is disturbing. These atheists embrace a belief system as intolerant, chauvinistic and bigoted as that of religious fundamentalists. They propose a route to collective salvation and the moral advancement of the human species through science and

reason. . . . All too often throughout history, those who believed in the possibility of this perfection (variously defined) have called for the silencing or eradication of human beings who are impediments to human progress. They turn their particular notion of the good into an inflexible standard of universal good. They prove blind to their own corruption and capacity for evil. They soon commit evil not for evil's sake but to make a better world.[7]

Similarly, Reza Aslan wrote the following in a column for the *Washington Post*:

There is, as has often been noted, something peculiarly evangelistic about what has been termed the new atheist movement. . . . It is no exaggeration to describe the movement popularized by the likes of Richard Dawkins, Daniel Dennett, Sam Harris, and Christopher Hitchens as a new and particularly zealous form of fundamentalism—an atheist fundamentalism. The parallels with religious fundamentalism are obvious and startling: the conviction that they are in sole possession of truth (scientific or otherwise), the troubling lack of tolerance for the views of their critics (Dawkins has compared creationists to Holocaust deniers), the insistence on a literalist reading of scripture (more literalist, in fact, than one finds among most religious fundamentalists), the simplistic reductionism of the religious phenomenon, and, perhaps most bizarrely, their overwhelming sense of siege: the belief that they have been oppressed and marginalized by Western societies and are just not going to take it anymore.[8]

Neither of these writers gets it *exactly* right. After spending several years deeply embedded in the atheist movement, I know there is no consensus on atheism, nor do I think that the intolerance that proliferates in the atheist movement is equivalent to religious extremism. (Though whenever I hear fellow atheists defend the intolerance among atheists by saying that it pales in comparison to the violence of religious extremists, I always think to myself: "Those are pretty meager standards to hold yourself up against.") The loudest voices are the most obvious, and it can be difficult to hear anyone else over their clamor—but the movement's emphasis on critical thinking does allow it to escape some of the trappings of actual fundamentalism. And the problem of loud, intolerant voices eclipsing voices of moderation and inclusion isn't one exclusive to the atheist movement.

However, both Aslan and Hedges make cogent points worth considering when they address the seeming arrogance and antagonism of the atheist movement—especially considering how it is perceived by those outside of it.

The way some folks on both sides talk about it, you'd think there was a cosmic war afoot. I've observed an innumerable number of bigoted comments on the American Atheists Facebook page and even violent propositions that we need to form an "atheist militia" to combat the religious and "burn down churches and synagogues." More and more, prominent atheist bloggers such as PZ Myers utilize violent imagery, like when he wrote this about people who believe in intelligent design:

> I say, screw the polite words and careful rhetoric. It's time for scientists to break out the steel-toed boots and brass knuckles, and get out there and hammer on the lunatics and idiots.[9]

PZ Myers is one of the most popular atheist bloggers in the world, and he has been one of the most persistent critics of my work (and of me personally). In early 2012, he and I were invited to participate in a public panel discussion on interfaith work for an official Fringe event of the Global Atheist Convention in Melbourne, Australia, with Leslie Cannold. In our discussion, Myers declared that the religious are "a bunch of extreme assholes" who have "something wrong with their brains" and in order to build up the atheist movement, we need to employ "us versus them" tactics against the religious. When he was asked when these in-group versus out-group walls would come down, he replied: "The walls will come down when religion is eradicated."[10]

To be sure, atheists aren't entirely to blame for this extreme "us versus them" mentality between the religious and nonreligious. There are many among the religious who do atheists the same disservice. We've become the bogeymen and bogeywomen, frequently used as a rallying point for the Religious Right. Historically speaking, the term "secular humanism" was actually popularized as an epithet against atheists.[11]

Today, atheist demonization is astoundingly common. For example, in the wake of the horrific shooting of Arizona congresswoman Gabrielle Giffords, in 2011, one right-wing pundit wrote: "When God is not in your life, evil will seek to fill the void."[12]

That same week, CNN commentator Erick Erickson attacked President Obama for making the national moment of silence in the wake of the shooting a time for "prayer or reflection."[13] Erickson accused the president of "accommodating atheists" and even used the example of the moment of silence as an opportunity to question Obama's faith. "That things like this keep coming up suggests the general public is right in their skepticism of the sincerity of his faith," said Erickson. In other words, any Christian who advocates for atheist inclusion isn't a real Christian. No wonder few speak out against comments like Erickson's.

Sadly, remarks like these aren't seen by most Americans as extraordinary—in fact, they're common currency. Not long after National Public Radio's Juan Williams was let go for making controversial remarks about Muslims, Erickson's remarks about atheists hardly inspired a murmur.

I hope that defending the nonreligious against rhetorical attacks like those made in the wake of this tragedy will become as instinctual as responding to those directed at our Muslim, Jewish, or Hindu neighbors. But, more generally, I hope more people will begin to act as watchdogs for rhetoric that demeans or diminishes any of our fellow humans, regardless of their religious or nonreligious identity.

So often when we talk about morality and ethics in the United States, we speak of religion in the same breath. As someone who's been working as an interfaith activist for several years, I get invited to participate in a good number of initiatives that use a common language of "faith" to motivate people and establish the religious as somehow set apart and differently motivated than the rest of the world. While such initiatives usually have the best of intentions, they run the risk of implicitly demeaning those who do not associate with a religious tradition.

Until those of us who do not believe in God are seen as having an equal capacity to be moral, anti-atheist remarks will continue to perpetuate discrimination and atheists will be seen as less moral than the religious.

—⁓—

The conversation around engagement between the religious and the nonreligious is a pressing issue in the atheist movement, and it is coming to a head. It began to get wider notice in late 2010, when the *New York Times* profiled the atheist movement and declared in a headline: "Atheists Debate How Pushy To Be."

The question continues to loom over the movement; every atheist or Humanist conference I've attended has had at least one talk or panel weighing the pros and cons of "confrontationalism" and "accommodationism," and it is debated on a near-weekly basis on the atheist blogosphere. In late 2011, prominent atheist Greta Christina brought the issue to light in an important blog post titled "What Are the Goals of the Atheist Movement?"

"I don't think all atheists—even all atheist activists—have the same goals," she wrote. "And I think this may be the source of some of this conflict and debate that we're having."[14] Simply put: there are competing and often contradictory goals among self-identified "atheist activists."

In an attempt to get at the heart of these conflicts, Christina named two goals of atheist activists. The first is one I share: "to see atheists be fully accepted into society, and to have our atheism recognized as legitimate." The second is one I do not: the demise of religion.

I take issue with the idea that atheist activism should consist of "persuading more people out of religion and into atheism," as Christina wrote. I work to promote critical thinking, education, religious liberty, compassion, and pluralism, and to fight tribalism, xenophobia, and fanaticism. Many religious people are allies to me and other atheists in these efforts—and a good number of them cite their religious convictions as the motivating factor behind their work. I am far more concerned about whether people are pluralistic in their worldview—if they oppose totalitarianism and believe those of different religious and nonreligious identities should be free to live as they choose and cooperate around shared values—than I am about whether someone believes in God or not.

Furthermore, I am deeply concerned about the way in which a growing number of atheists engage in "confrontationalism," defined by Christina as "arguing with believers about religion, or making fun of it, or insulting it." Focusing one's activism on criticizing a caricature of religion does nothing to improve atheism's image; in fact, it actively hampers attempts to improve the conditions of life for nonreligious people. Criticizing intolerant beliefs and practices is vitally important, but unsophisticated criticisms of religion en masse estrange reasonable people—both fellow atheists and potential religious allies.

In her writing, Christina has frequently pointed to the successes of the gay rights movement, saying that in order to succeed as the gay rights movement has, the atheist movement needs both kind atheists and hostile ones, both "diplomats and firebrands."[15] But there is an important difference that makes this a far from perfect parallel: the "confrontationalists" of the gay rights movement were working to fight against heterosexism and legally supported discrimination and bias against queer people, but they weren't trying to eliminate heterosexuality. Christina and many others in the atheist movement claim that they are working to eliminate religion, which is a very different fight than working toward freedom of—and freedom from—religion.

Thus, I believe *how pushy should we be?* is the wrong question. Do we simply want to eradicate religion, or do we want to improve the world? I realize that for many these aims aren't mutually exclusive, but surely the latter must be our *ultimate* aim. There are profound disagreements about whether or not the former will accomplish the latter, though looking at secular societies that have experienced genocide and war, it is clear that tribalism—behavior and attitudes that stem from strong loyalty to one's own tribe or social group—is the primary problem. A world absent of religion would not necessarily be a more cooperative or peaceful one; a world absent of fanaticism, totalitarianism, and tribalism would certainly be.

—ɯ—

I've learned a lot in the time I've been deeply invested in the athe-ist community, and I believe that in many cases it is actually more challenging for atheists to get involved in interfaith work because of cultural factors. One study, from 2010, found that atheists in the United States are less agreeable and less conscientious than the religious—but that the factors responsible were largely cul-tural, and atheists' minority position in American society played a significant role in this being so.[16] Being a member of an intensely disliked religious minority in a culture that privileges Christian-ity in particular and religiosity more generally makes respectful engagement more challenging; for atheists, a widely disliked and often reviled group, it often isn't as simple as just sitting down at a table and saying hello.

During the last several years I've met nontheists from all over; their stories have given me perspective on the difficulties some atheists face in day-to-day life. And yet, as sensitive as I am to these realities, they actually confirm what I believe about respectful en-gagement. Because there are so few atheists, because atheists are so distrusted, and because antireligious appeals currently constitute the movement's primary form out of outreach, positive interaction with the religious is desperately needed.

When I go out and speak with religious individuals and com-munities about atheism, the most common feedback I get is that many people have had very negative experiences with atheists. I hasten to reassure them that the majority of atheists are just like everyone else—kind, generous, interested in living lives of mean-ing and purpose—and that the image of atheists as mean-spirited, nihilistic, and intolerant is a stereotype. But the increasingly vocal and vitriolic subset of the atheist community has made my work of persuading people to abandon their negative preconceptions of atheists a lot more difficult, and it makes it possible for religious people who don't know many or any atheists to tokenize me and others doing similar work—to see us as the exceptions, to see me as the "one good atheist." This is the opposite of what I and others are trying to accomplish, and it frustrates me that some atheists enable and perpetuate the widespread mistrust of atheists.

There are many possible answers to the question of how atheists should engage with the religious, but we will be no closer to the answer if we merely continue to debate it—and we will never answer it if we isolate ourselves from religious communities. We must engage. We may not know with certainty the best way to go about cooperation between the religious and the nonreligious, but the problems of the world are too numerous to debate it for long. We must find solidarity wherever we can—and act upon it.

I definitely don't always get this right, but I'm trying to practice what I preach the best that I can. It helps me to ask in any given situation that begins to move into conflict: What am I doing to contribute to the problem? What are the implicit desires grounding my actions in this moment, and am I acknowledging my own intentions? A bit of intellectual humility and self-awareness goes a long way; a quick perusal of human history shows that when one person's idea of "rationality" trumps basic human decency for others, we all suffer.

Let's learn from our shared past and imagine, together, a more vibrant future. I'm tired of seeing people pitted against one another because of these inherently false broad strokes that paint religious people as "delusional" and atheists as "degenerates." Let's start to see one another as people first.

In the next chapter, I will lay out some of what I've learned about atheists and interfaith work. It is meant to be an introduction;

this is still a growing field, and there is much work to be done. And, as it has been for most of my life, I'd like to explore it alongside others, in community.

—⁓—

As I was preparing to leave Chicago to start my work at the Humanist Chaplaincy at Harvard, I was intentional about saying good-bye to all the good friends I had made during my two and a half years there. On one of my final nights in the city, I went out with a dear friend I had met in one of my master's program religion classes. We went to a gay bar—I was his first close gay friend and we had found a small neighborhood bar just a block from his apartment that we enjoyed visiting because it maintained a remarkably diverse patronage.

While we were there, a Christian man approached us. Admitting that he had been eavesdropping on our conversation, he asked why I, as an atheist, would get involved in interfaith work. We ended up discussing a whole range of topics, from the possibility of an afterlife to our favorite beers, and at one point he posited a question: "Okay, but tell me this, Mr. Atheist: Where did we come from? How did all of this get here?"

I answered: "Well, I'm not a scientist"—a line I often offer with a chuckle when I'm confronted with a question to which I don't know the answer, which happens, well, often—"but to be honest, that question doesn't matter all that much to me. Investigating humanity's origins is an important endeavor, but as far as I'm concerned there's a more urgent question. What concerns me, given that we are here, is what will we do?"

A year later, famed theoretical physicist Stephen Hawking made headlines when he said during an interview that he didn't believe in an afterlife. But in my mind, the most pivotal moment of that interview was also the most overlooked. In a blink-and-you'll-miss-it sentence, Hawking offered an imperative call to action:

Q: So here we are. What should we do?

A: We should seek the greatest value of our action.[17]

Given that we are here, what will we do? What is the greatest value of our action? I'm not a scientist, but I believe the answer is as simple as seeking to understand the diverse people who are here with us, and working together to advance equality and justice for all.

8

Fact or Friction,
Engage or Enrage

I have made a ceaseless effort not to ridicule, not to bewail,
not to scorn human actions, but to understand them.

—Baruch Spinoza

I've questioned the appropriateness of writing a memoir before
reaching the age of twenty-five more than a few times. In many
ways, it feels a bit silly, if not premature, to rehash my past. I'm
more concerned with questions of my present—occupying myself
with thoughts of how I'm living in and contributing to the world
around me—than I am with revisiting identities I used to inhabit
or beliefs I've since renounced.

Yet surveying the trajectory I've taken offers some instruc-
tive revelations. First, there is a significant parallel between the
certitude I felt as a conflicted, fundamentalist Christian and as a
conflicted, antireligious atheist. Both represented my desire for
certainty, but both came at the expense of others' humanity.

Second, my life-long search for meaning has been a journey
of navigating identity. But for much of it, I didn't bring my full self
to the table—first when I was closeted in the Christian community
and, later, when I was biased against religious people because of
the emotional injuries I sustained and my reluctance to broach the
subject of religious differences in my relationships. Because I was

unable and unwilling to be honest about who I was, I was guarded. The walls I built didn't really protect me, though; instead, they inhibited me from seeing others as full human beings, and they prevented others from knowing me and challenging their assumptions about queer people and atheists. I looked for the negative to confirm my preexisting biases, instead of supporting and advocating for positive change or making sense of my own desires and values. And because I was always looking for a fight, for enemies to defend myself against, I had a difficult time seeing the good in those who seemed different.

The activism of my adolescence was defined by self-righteousness, such as when I camped out in front of a conference on anti-gay "reparative therapy" and shouted at those going in, high-fiving my fellow activists every time someone cowered or averted his gaze. I took a kind of pleasure in making people uncomfortable and tried to adopt the "I don't give a fuck" posture I saw others employ. If people didn't accept me for who I was—immediately, in totality, and without flinching—then they could go fuck themselves, right? It wasn't my job to coddle them into being tolerant or to make them feel okay about their inability to do so.

Over the years, I learned how to meet people in the middle or even further, and, all the more, to see people as individuals instead of members of categories I didn't belong to. Rather than casting those who disagree with me as steadfast adversaries, I have come to see them as complex human beings and our interactions as opportunities to learn and grow together. This shift in perspective has enabled me to make peace with the struggles of my past, and the activism-by-fist of my younger years has gradually transformed into an extended arm of invitation.

Directing anger at others can feel good, but I've found that a hangover follows. On the contrary, I've never regretted responding to intolerance with love. As Martin Luther King Jr. wrote:

The ultimate weakness of violence is that it is a descending spiral, begetting the very thing it seeks to destroy. Instead of diminishing evil, it multiplies it. Through violence you murder the hater, but you do not murder hate. . . . Returning violence for violence multiplies violence, adding deeper darkness to a night already devoid of stars. Darkness cannot drive out darkness; only light can do that. Hate cannot drive out hate; only love can do that.[1]

He was only twenty-six when he partnered with people of all beliefs and backgrounds to organize the Montgomery bus boycott. As a twentysomething, I'm sure King entertained the question: "Who am I?" But when I think of how he lived, a larger question looms for me about Humanists and about all of us: "Who can we be together?"

Still, knowing your own story is the first step. As Alasdair Macintyre said: "I can only answer the question, 'What am I to do?' if I can answer the prior question, 'Of what story or stories do I find myself a part?'"[2] The question of self informs the answer of how one situates oneself in the world. But though the question of self may never be fully answered, the urgency of learning how to love one another is too great to put off.

I look at my life now and am astonished by much has changed since the days I earnestly believed I was spiritually sick; that fearful eleven-year-old boy who went to church for the free pizza and because he was looking for somewhere to belong has developed into a young man who is comfortable enough in his own skin to take the risk of reaching out to others. Where there was once an uncertain, frightened, self-protective, and angry young boy, there is now someone focused on building understanding with the hope that someday no one will be marginalized because of who they are. These lives—the child I was and the, dare I say it, adult that I am—feel disconnected in all the obvious ways, but they are connected by a thread of growth, a move from being guided by fear and anger to curiosity and empathy. The changes in my life, the shift from insecurity to balance, are the direct result of the understanding I have found from and with other people; from seeking, discovering, and creating spaces where I could relearn how to be myself, where I could introduce my authentic self to strangers after years of hiding, and where I could invite others to teach me about our differences.

For years I was blinded by my own anger, animosity, and resentment. It prevented me from seeing myself honestly, and from seeing and hearing others in their complexity. My indiscriminate desire to pick fights made me look for the worst in others and ignore the nuance. My defensiveness seized any opportunity to imagine myself under siege. That negative outlook—where everyone who didn't think like me was probably my enemy—became the lens through which I viewed the world.

I've still got a mean streak. The kid who lived to provoke my siblings, who once made a "suggestion box" out of an empty tissue holder in the middle of a high school math class for a bungling, ineffectual first-year teacher and passed it around the room—that occasionally rude rabble-rouser still lives in me. But I have found more productive uses for that energy, for my desire to challenge and change.

Similarly, the confidence I lost during the years I spent beating myself up for who I was has returned, but it is different now. It is tempered, it is cautious and protective, and I like to think it is humble. The toned-down nature of my confidence allows me to love in ways I couldn't before: to let things happen on terms other than my own, to trust in the potential goodness of others, to derive satisfaction from another's happiness, to reach out and try to meet people where they are. And in a universe where I believe meaning and purpose are not gifted from a divine source but are instead collectively assembled by humans, learning to live alongside and love others—all others—is perhaps our greatest task.

I wrote this book because I want to live in a world where love is more commonplace, and the way I'm trying to do that is by working to advance the conversation on how atheists and the religious relate to one another. Sharing my experiences is the best way I know how to do that. There are many other stories I could tell from the years I've dedicated to this work—the atheist students I've met who sheepishly admitted they've never talked to their religious classmates about their beliefs; the religious students I've met who admitted they had negative stereotypes about atheists and vowed to challenge them; the people who are pushing religious communities into a pluralistic mindset; the allies all across Boston who work with me every day in interfaith solidarity to fight hunger, anti-gay and anti-Muslim intolerance, and other affronts to human dignity. But I know my own story better than any other, so that's where I've begun.

My experiences have led me to the conclusion that atheists and the religious need to find better ways to talk to one another, and they need to identify the areas of shared humanity that will enable mutually enriching collaboration. For the last several years, I've explored this with people of faith and with atheists. Although my advice on how to advance this conversation is limited, I can say with unwavering confidence that it is an endeavor worth pursuing, and I encourage others to try it for themselves.

That said, I've got a few ideas.

—⁊⁊—

Religious pluralism is neither coexistence nor consensus. Interfaith Youth Core's Eboo Patel and Cassie Meyer write: "Drawing from Harvard scholar Diana Eck, IFYC articulates religious pluralism as the active engagement of religious diversity to a constructive end.

Diversity is a mere descriptive fact; 'pluralism is an achievement' (Eck). We break this definition further into three essential components: respect for individual religious or non-religious identity, mutually inspiring relationships, and common action for the common good."[3]

Interfaith dialogue strives to usher in religious pluralism, and it is realized primarily through the personal stories of its practitioners. Storytelling aids dialogue because it is nonthreatening, because it prompts a mutual exchange of stories that help people bond, and because it allows people to talk about their identities in a way that feels safe. By grounding dialogue in individual experience, the listener is less likely to be offended by what might be alien to her or his own experience. Instead of provoking a negative response, IFYC suggests that this exchange can result in mutually inspiring relationships and common action:

> In interfaith dialogue, it is far too easy to discuss topics that may put us at odds with our conversation partners. . . . If, however, we encourage participants to begin with a story from their own lived experience, it is often less threatening for listeners. While they may not have lived the same experience as the storyteller, it is unlikely that they will challenge the veracity of his or her own story. Instead, the storyteller is inviting the listeners to share in a piece of his or her own experience, even if it is grounded in different beliefs or values. The dialogue is therefore inclusive rather than exclusive and allows for a mutually appreciative encounter.[4]

As the above selection indicates, before one can become an active agent of engaging religious pluralism, an individual must be grounded in her or his own particular identity. This of course presents two intriguing questions: How might nonreligious individuals participate in a movement encouraging engaged religious pluralism that is rooted in particular religious identity? And why should we?

There are four primary reasons that engaging in interfaith work will benefit the nonreligious, which I will expand on below: we're outnumbered; we want to end religious extremism and other forms of oppression and suffering; we have a lot to learn; and we have a bad reputation and are discriminated against.

1. Atheists Are Outnumbered, aka the Pragmatic Argument

Whether we wish to or not, atheists are forced by proximity to engage with the religious. It seems implausible that any nonreligious person in America has strictly secular relationships. We're outnumbered. Though the number of Americans who do not identify with any religion is growing, atheism remains a minority perspective. More interestingly, American religious communities are undergoing some interesting shifts that, try as some atheists might, make it impossible for us to approach them as a monolithic and inert community that is strictly problematic.

As I noted in the first chapter, survey data demonstrates that religion is unlikely to lose its social influence in the conceivable future. Though young Americans are significantly less likely than older generations to claim religious membership or attend a religious service regularly, religion continues to permeate American life—it seems that the majority of the religiously unaffiliated still maintain religious or supernatural beliefs, while religious fundamentalism is experiencing renewed growth both domestically and around the world.

Though religion today looks very different than it has in the past, it isn't about to vanish from the face of the earth. And since people of faith are our neighbors, we ought to know them and their motivations. In giving them an opportunity to get to know us and the stories of our experiences as nonreligious persons—and, perhaps more importantly, not forgetting to get to know them—we will begin to erode some of the divisions between the secular and the religious. By doing so we are likely, as IFYC suggests, to identify some shared values upon which we can act in interfaith solidarity. The interfaith coalition that led the American civil rights movement recognized that success would require respecting the many different reasons people come to the table to support a common cause. Unless we strive to understand people's religious beliefs and practices, efforts that hinge on solidarity will fail. Without knowing and understanding the spectrum of moral and religious beliefs that compel people to act, we will remain divided.

You don't even need to think that religion can be a positive force in the world to see the value in interfaith cooperation that includes the nonreligious. As citizens of a religiously diverse world, interfaith cooperation is a necessity in order to accomplish things that require a coalition larger than the community to which you belong—whether you wish to see religion come to an end or not.

2. We Want to End Religious Extremism and Other Forms of Oppression and Suffering, aka the Shared-Values Argument

One such common goal shared by the interfaith cooperation movement and the atheist movement is a proactive aim to end religious extremism. The interfaith movement is inherently rooted in an antifundamentalism framework. In *Acts of Faith*, Eboo Patel writes that "the twenty-first century will be shaped by the question of the faith line. On one side of the faith line are the religious totalitarians. Their conviction is that only one interpretation of one religion is a legitimate way of being, believing, and belonging on earth. Everyone else needs to be cowed, or converted, or condemned, or killed. On the other side of the faith line are the religious pluralists, who hold that people believing in different creeds and belonging to different communities need to learn to live together."[5]

Atheists and the nonreligious ought to see ourselves as having a lot in common with religious pluralists; likewise, religious pluralists are likely to see themselves as having more in common with us than with the extremists who also claim their tradition. In allying our efforts to combat religious extremism with likeminded campaigns occurring within religious communities, our efforts will be more effective. A Muslim speaking out against religious extremism will probably be better received by Muslim communities than a Humanist.

In *Ethnic Conflict and Civic Life: Hindus and Muslims in India*, political scientist Ashutosh Varshney noted that the likelihood that inciting events will lead to widespread or long-term violence is significantly less in communities where civic ties across lines of identity differentiation were present. In populations where such ties were nonexistent, inciting incidents provoked extensive interidentity violence. Thus, as interfaith cooperation asserts, invested relationships across lines of identity difference are essential for avoiding conflict.

One of the top priorities of organized secular communities is criticizing and combating religiously based oppression, and pluralistic religious communities can be among our strongest allies in this work. However, if we adopt a broadly negative approach to religion and religious communities, we may burn these bridges and lose the opportunity to count these communities as allies.

3. We Have a Lot to Learn, aka the Educational Argument

These mutual interests can never be identified if we fail to recognize that religious communities have a lot to teach us. In "E Pluribus Unum: Diversity and Community in the 21st Century," Robert

Putnam wrote that diversity is important to building strong and sustainable communities. But, at least at first, people tend to "hunker down" with those very similar to themselves and gaze upon newcomers with suspicion. For diversity to flower, individuals must meet and learn from one another.

A quote from Carl Sagan appears at the very beginning of this book, and I'd like to think that some of his ideas permeate this work. The pragmatism, compassion, curiosity, and creativity that he modeled in his life and in his work inspire me to live a life that both acknowledges truth and prioritizes kindness toward others. As he once wrote: "Every one of us is, in the cosmic perspective, precious. If a human disagrees with you, let him live. In a hundred billion galaxies, you will not find another."[6]

While I agree with that sentiment, I'd like to go a step further. I don't want to just let those who disagree with me live— I want to go out of my way to try to befriend and understand them. Sure enough, some of my greatest insights have grown out of such relationships.

We can also learn from and adapt the best that religious communities have to offer, as Alain de Botton argued in *Religion for Atheists: A Non-Believer's Guide to the Uses of Religion*. Some nonreligious communities and individuals utilize so-called religious practices—for example, the Harvard Humanist Contemplative Group runs well-attended meditation sessions. There are Humanist chaplains. Humanist celebrants perform invocations, weddings, baby-naming ceremonies, and funerals. Some lift heavily from religious traditions, even if that just involves looking to the best practices of successful religious communities.

Furthermore, many religions have nurtured activists and antioppression movements. Many of history's greatest advocates for the disenfranchised—Rev. Dr. Martin Luther King Jr., Mahatma

Gandhi, Thich Nhat Hanh, Rabbi Abraham Joshua Heschel, Msgr. Oscar Romero, and many others—cited their religious convictions as the primary impetus for their social justice work and launched their efforts in interfaith coalitions. And though some secular individuals cast religion as an inherently bad thing, it is not difficult to make a case that aspects of religion have been and continue to be a force for good in the world. There is a storied history of religious social justice, and we would do well to learn from it; religiously based social justice continues in great force today, and we would do well to join with it. This will require a willingness to learn from people, even if we think some of their beliefs are incorrect.

It is also important to remember that religious criticism is not the exclusive domain of the nonreligious, and acting like it is by adopting a "religious people versus atheists" mentality while painting all religious believers with a broad brush alienates allies in the important fight against dogmatism and totalitarianism. Criticism of religious beliefs isn't a new thing; its legacy is as long as the existence of religion itself, and it rests of the backs of outspoken religious leaders like Martin Luther, Mahatma Gandhi, Martin Luther King Jr., and even the biblical Jesus Christ. But they—like many religious critics today who work within their own communities— were reformers, not abolitionists.

Regardless of whether you find anything in religion admirable, it seems that, for now anyway, religion is unlikely to become irrelevant. And in a world where religious conflict is in the headlines on a daily basis and religious illiteracy is widespread, it actually feels increasingly relevant. The dangers of acting like it isn't are clear: when fraught issues related to religion arise, being unable to contextualize them or understand their implications makes it difficult to know how to respond. Cultivating positive relationships between people of diverse religious and nonreligious identities not only helps prevent conflict by creating invested relationships—it also combats ignorance by giving people the opportunity to educate one another about their beliefs and backgrounds.

4. We Have a Bad Reputation and Are Discriminated Against, aka the Necessity Argument

If we do not allow others to know us by intentionally engaging diversity, we lose an opportunity to ensure that our own rights are protected. More generally, the respectful relationships we establish with religious communities will also help us reinforce a positive public image for nontheists.

I have seen the dividends of this firsthand time and time again, and it has largely resulted from my work with people who claim not to know many atheists. Because we represent such a small sliver of the American population—and, as noted in the previous chapter, because we are often seen in a negative light—it is imperative that atheists make themselves known. A 2010 Gallup poll demonstrated something the LGBTQ community has recognized for some time: people are significantly more inclined to oppose gay marriage if they do not know anyone who is gay.[7] Similarly, a *Time* magazine cover story that same year featured revealing numbers that speak volumes about the correlation between positive relationships and civic support; per their survey, 46 percent of Americans think Islam is more violent than other faiths, and 61 percent oppose Park51 (or the "Ground Zero Mosque"), but only 37 percent even know a Muslim American.[8] Another survey released around the same time, by Pew, reported that 55 percent of Americans know "not very much" or "nothing at all" about Islam. The disconnect is clear: when only 37 percent of Americans know a Muslim American, and 55 percent claim to know very little or nothing about Islam, the negative stereotypes about the Muslim community go unchallenged.[9] The same logic can be extended to atheists—the fewer relationships we have with people of faith, the worse our image will be. By building coalitions and letting ourselves be known by the religious, we will deconstruct the stereotypes imposed upon us and ensure our protection and respect from others.

Based on my experiences as an atheist and an interfaith activist, I have confidence that building relationships of mutuality and respect will alter the negative public perceptions about atheists. As Abraham Lincoln once said:

> If you would win a man to your cause, first convince him that you are his sincere friend. Therein is a drop of honey that catches his heart, which, say what he will, is the great high road to his reason, and which, when once gained, you will find but little trouble in convincing his judgment of the justice of your cause, if indeed that cause really be a just one. On the contrary, assume to dictate to his judgment, or to command his action, or to mark him as one to be shunned and despised, and he will retreat within himself, close all the avenues to his head and his heart; and tho' your cause be naked truth itself, transformed to the heaviest lance, harder than steel, and sharper than steel can be made, and tho' you throw it with more than Herculean force and precision, you shall no more be able to pierce him, than to penetrate the hard shell of a tortoise with a rye straw.[10]

TWO MAJOR CRITIQUES

Since I started writing and speaking about interfaith work, I've read a significant amount of criticism of atheists participating in these efforts. From this writing it seems a large percentage of atheist interfaith opponents have kept their distance from interfaith work. I understand their hesitation, but I can't help wondering if

there is some disconnect when those who most heavily criticize
the interfaith movement also seem to have had little to no actual
experience with it. I could be wrong, but I'd be surprised if someone who had been involved in interfaith work would suggest, as
PZ Myers did, that it "cheerfully and indiscriminately embrace[s]
every faith without regard for content."[11]

Almost every argument I've read or heard from atheists opposed to interfaith work employs two critiques, and they're directly
related: that interfaith leaves no room for religious criticism, and
that it by default excludes atheists because atheism isn't a "faith."
Atheists' rejection of interfaith work seems to be due in large part
to an underlying assumption that, in order to participate, everyone
must bite his or her tongue and play nice, and that participation in
this kind of movement lends our implicit approval to "faith" as a
concept and rallying point.

Unsurprisingly, the idea that interfaith work requires significant tongue-biting makes many atheists very uncomfortable; it
was certainly a concern I had before I started working in the interfaith movement. The irony of this worry is that the atheist and
interfaith movements actually share a common point of origin:
they both started, in part, as a reaction to religious extremism.
Much like the atheist movement, the interfaith movement seeks
to build intergroup understanding, encourage critical thinking,
and end religiously based social and political exclusivism. The
fundamental misunderstanding many people have is imagining
that the interfaith movement is uninterested in combating religious totalitarianism and that it exists solely to maintain religious
privilege—as an excuse to show that religion, in its many diverse
forms, owns morality.

This concern couldn't be further from the truth. In fact, atheists participating in interfaith programs actually disrupt religious
privilege by asserting that, for us, religious beliefs have little or

nothing to do with our ethics. But if atheists do not participate in ongoing interfaith efforts, we leave the field open for the idea that faith is the only driving factor that compels people to work for a better world. By opting not to participate, atheists leave the ground uncontested for people of faith to claim. But by showing up, atheists demonstrate that religion does not have a monopoly on morality.

In my experience, interfaith work exists to eliminate religious privilege by bringing diverse religious and nonreligious people into common work to build relationships that might deconstruct the kind of "us versus them" thinking that contributes to exclusivist religious hierarchy. It is a place to challenge and question but to do so constructively.

The success of such challenges is contingent on whether invested relationships exist between the involved parties. If not, disagreements run the risk of degenerating into shouting matches in place of reasonable discourse. Though in the United States atheists and the religious don't regularly commit physical violence against one another, it is clear that invested relationships across lines of identity difference are essential for cooperation and constructive intergroup communication, whether those groups are religious or not.

Whether engaging Christians around my negative experiences as a former evangelical and as a queer person, or challenging my religious peers to explain their beliefs rationally, I've found interfaith work to not only be a fruitful place for such conversations but, in fact, the ideal forum for it. I can fondly recall any number of incidents when I argued theology and philosophy with religious colleagues while doing interfaith work and how, later, they told me that they actually took my perspective seriously because we had built a trusting relationship. It made all the difference that I treated them as intellectual equals—as people with respectable goals rather than just mindless adherents of some stupid religion. They had heard positions similar to mine in the past from other atheists, but the arguments had been presented so disrespectfully that they made no impact, and in some cases closed my religious colleagues to even entertaining such ideas.

This is precisely what interfaith work sets out to do: elicit civil dialogue to increase understanding, not stifle it for the sake of "playing nice."

There is a related concern many atheists have about joining interfaith coalitions: that participating in this work somehow bolsters religious privilege. And, all the more, that some people will conflate atheists participating in interfaith work with the idea that atheism is "just another religion," when some of the underlying values of a religious mindset are exactly what many atheists reject.

I can only speak from my experience here, but I have been invited to address interfaith conferences and groups many times, and I often open with this line: "Let's get one thing out of the way— atheism and Humanism aren't religions." Not once have I had anyone disagree with me.

I fully acknowledge that the language of "interfaith" is imperfect, clunky, and can feel exclusive to many nonreligious people. But I think we should participate in interfaith efforts anyway. Interfaith is currently the most-recognized term to describe activities that bring the religious and nonreligious together for dialogue and common work; it is used far and wide by many, including the Obama administration. (When President Obama announced his Interfaith and Community Service Campus Challenge, he specifically highlighted the nonreligious as key stakeholders in this work.)[12]

I believe that change will come from within—that by participating in interfaith work, the nonreligious will broaden the meaning of such efforts and that the language used to describe them will change accordingly. This has certainly been true of my experiences in the interfaith movement—when I first began, the language was often quite religious-centric. But in just a few years, it has shifted dramatically to include the nonreligious. One example is an interfaith organization I have collaborated with in Massachusetts that fights homelessness. When I first began to work with them, they went by the name Social Action Ministries. Soon, however, we began a discussion about their name. Before long, they decided to change it to Social Action Massachusetts. In a guest post for my blog about this decision, their coordinator, Caitlin Golden, wrote: "We don't want to be just inter*faith*—our dialogue and our action will only be truly inclusive if they also include the voices of those who do not identify with the *faith* part of interfaith at all. This isn't about 'watering down' the conversation to a lowest common denominator or pretending that we're all in theological or philosophical agreement, but rather about creating the space for people of diverse identities to share the values that lead them to engage in social action."[13]

To atheists concerned about being seen as "just another faith" and worried that interfaith isn't an avenue for substantive discourse: I encourage you to give it a shot anyway, and be vocal about where you stand. I cannot begin to recount all of the times interfaith work has opened up a space for robust conversations on problematic religious practices and beliefs. In fact, it has been a hallmark of my experience working in the interfaith movement. Furthermore, it has allowed me to engage religious people about atheist identity and eradicate significant misconceptions about what atheism is and what it isn't.

I regularly hear from atheists who are leading the charge for interfaith cooperation on their campuses and in their communities, and their experiences echo mine. They too have found that interfaith is expanding to incorporate them and that, when done well, interfaith engagement doesn't require that people check their convictions at the door; it invites people to try to understand and humanize the other.

It's a worthy goal—a necessary one—and if the only thing keeping some atheists from participating is a disagreement with the term "interfaith," then that is a missed opportunity.

—⚬⚬—

"I still can't believe this is what I do for living," I thought to myself as I walked out of the airport in State College, Pennsylvania.

I was met by the Reverend David Witkovsky, campus chaplain for Juniata College in Huntingdon and Campus Ministry intern Lauren Seganos. They climbed out of a blue car and gave me a giant hug. "Welcome to rural Pennsylvania," said Lauren as the crisp April wind threatened to knock us over.

I was in the middle of my second speaking tour of 2011. That night, I spoke at a small church that was working toward creating a "welcoming statement" for LGBT individuals. I shared my current beliefs and work, and discussed some of my experiences as a queer person and a former Christian—experiences of being alienated from my church, of being physically assaulted by a group of men shouting Bible verses at me, but also moments of radical welcoming—and I listened to them as they detailed the struggle within their community around this issue. We learned a lot about one another, and I left feeling very encouraged by their desire to make their church a safe space for all people.

I kicked off the next day by speaking in a World Religions class about atheism, Humanism, and the religiously unaffiliated. After my remarks a student approached me, speaking in a small whisper. "I'm an atheist," she said. "I feel isolated, and most of the atheist community I find online is largely about bashing religious people.

I've wanted to find a positive community, and I want to be open about my atheism. Thanks for starting this conversation here."

Exchanges like that continued throughout the day—after a public discussion on Humanism that I facilitated, during meetings with students and staff—and when it was finally time for my evening speech on atheism and interfaith cooperation, the lecture hall was full to capacity. Students of all different backgrounds— Christians, atheists, Muslims, Jews, and others—had come together and offered questions, challenges, and their hope for positive dialogue, community, and action.

After my speech, a student who had attended nearly every event I was at that day came up to me and asked if we could talk sometime. I was exhausted from a full day, but I offered to meet him for coffee early the next morning before I had to catch a Megabus to Pittsburgh.

As the sun rose, we discussed the challenges of growing up queer in a conservative religious environment and of our shared hope for a world in which people seek out the good in one another. I tried to do more listening than talking and found myself hugely inspired by this student's optimism in the face of difficult life experiences. We finished with a hug and agreed to stay in touch.

Sitting on the bus that day, I felt more convinced than ever that interfaith work contains the potential to improve people's lives. I thought back to my meeting with the Juniata Interfaith Council the day before—to the atheists at the meeting who spoke about their commitment to inclusion and justice and about their desire to contribute to interfaith social action. By the meeting's end, we had identified concrete steps to create a Secular Student Alliance group for nonreligious students so that they too would have a community. The Campus Ministry office offered to support the students' efforts however they could.

There were a lot of atheist, agnostic, Humanist, and nonreligious students at Juniata who felt isolated—and now, thanks to the generous welcome of Juniata's Campus Ministry, they'll have a community of their own—and they've been affirmed as essential participants at the interfaith table. Now, there will be no empty chairs.

I still reflect on both the challenges and the hope expressed by the atheist and Humanist students I met at Juniata; of a retired Juniata religion professor who educated student after student about the world's many religions but who, as an atheist, never felt he could voice his own views and values; of religious students filled with love and admiration for their atheist friends; of the queer students I met with stories much like my own. I continue to be moved beyond measure by the people I encountered there, and by how bold the atheist and religious students I've encountered at Juniata and many other schools have been in their promise to work together.

Dialogue isn't meaningless—the humanization of the "other" elicited by an act of intentional encounter with difference leads to real change. Engaging in interfaith coalition-building efforts requires a certain level of vulnerability and humility; to be understood, we all must work to understand. To understand our privileges, our pasts, our prejudices, and what we each bring to the table in order to strengthen ourselves as a community and as a country, we must be willing to challenge the beliefs we have about those who seem different—and the result is often life-changing for all parties involved. Everyone I've met who has taken part in interfaith dialogue has walked away challenged, with a renewed sense of personal agency and a feeling of shared responsibility to bring about a more pluralistic world.

Communities like the one at Juniata, the community of Humanists and interfaith activists at Harvard, and the many others

I've encountered in my travels—where the mutual goals of love and service remain at the forefront of people's thoughts and actions—present a hope I long to see actualized in religious and nonreligious communities alike: for the sake of Humanism, and for the sake of all humans.

I looked out the window at Pennsylvania farmland, headed to another college for another speech, perpetually moving—but, for a moment, in the still and quiet of a softly rolling bus, I was filled with gratitude for the gift of the stories I heard, humbled by the commitment to inclusivity and action I had witnessed among Juniata's students and staff, and inspired to continue pushing for positive change.

I really can't believe this is what I do for living, *I thought.*
I doubt I ever will.

Afterword

I started this book with my childhood; I'd like to end where I began.

Whenever I get a little too proud or boastful or self-righteous about what I believe to be true about the world—and no matter how many times I try to adopt a humble and inquisitive stance, it's never too long before it happens—my mom recounts a story about me as a child.

It was my cousin Alex's birthday party and, after hours of party games and gift-opening, it was time for dessert. Enraptured by the excitement of the celebration, Alex ran up to me, his face covered in pink and orange and green, to share his joy with his one-year-older cousin.

"Isn't my birthday ice cream so good?!" he said, ecstatic.

Without pausing, I said matter-of-factly: "It isn't ice cream, Alex. It's sherbet."

My mom always laughs when she tells this story, adding that she is glad I'm lightening up a bit with age.

In my youth, being "right" held ultimacy. I valued precision and accuracy, and was sure to correct anyone I felt was "wrong." I thought I was doing people a favor by correcting them. Now, I strive to lead with listening instead of lecturing.

We can be dogmatically fixated on who is "right" and who is "wrong," or we can discern a way to live together in tension and ambiguity. Joining forces, we can buck the clash-of-civilizations story that has come to define our world and dictate a new narrative—one that bridges the religious and the secular, rather than threatening the "other" with extinction.

By reaching out to those who see things in a different way, we have the opportunity to write a new story about religious difference. In the words of Native novelist and scholar Thomas King: "The truth about stories is that that's all we are. . . . Want a different ethic? Tell a different story."[1]

It may sound overly simplistic, but I really do believe that the only way to begin writing this story is to tell our own and listen to those of others; to step boldly and defiantly across dividing lines of religious and nonreligious identity and share our experiences in hope that we might build understanding through relationships of commitment and cooperation.

I used to be afraid to speak out—for myself or on behalf of others. I was paralyzed by the fear that I wasn't old enough, that I didn't have the words, didn't know what to say, didn't understand communities I wasn't a member of, didn't know who I was, didn't have it all figured out.

I still don't have it all figured out. But there is one thing I know: in the face of innumerable, incomprehensible incidents of intolerance, hatred, and violence in this world over disagreements about the veracity of religious claims, the time is now to open up a dialogue. So I've started with the one thing I knew better than anything else: my story.

I've told mine—now it's your turn.

Do you want to take the next step but aren't sure how? Visit www
.faitheistbook.com for a downloadable resource with tips on how
to start building bridges between atheists and the religious!

—⚹—

The Trevor Project is the leading national organization providing
crisis intervention and suicide prevention services to lesbian, gay,
bisexual, transgender, and questioning young people under age
twenty-four. If you or a young person you care about needs support, call the Trevor Lifeline at 866-488-7386. It's free, confidential,
and available 24/7. Learn more at TheTrevorProject.org.

Acknowledgments

The rabbi Harold Kushner once said, "The challenge of being human is so great, no one gets it right every time." Here's to everyone who's helped me get it a little bit more right every day . . .

First and foremost, I need to thank my mother for guiding—and, at one point, saving—my life, and for being the best role model I could ever ask for. You are nearly everything I aspire to be, and I am so lucky to have you as a friend and role model. Though you don't figure into the book as prominently, my incredible siblings—Casi, Colton, and Cahlor—are present in every word I wrote; your love, support, and patience over the years can't be overemphasized. Whether it was Casi holding my hand as I prepared to come out to Teens Encounter Christ, Colton defending me to his football teammates when I was the only openly gay kid in our high school, or Cahlor speaking out in his church confirmation class during their sexuality unit, you've fearlessly gone to bat for me time and time again, and I am so grateful for your love. To Charlie and all of my aunts, uncles, cousins, grandparents, nieces, and nephews—I love and cherish each of you. To the members of my family who do not support me—I still hope for reconciliation. To my father—I love you; we'll get there.

Eboo Patel—I cannot begin to thank you for the inspiration, the opportunities, and your enthusiasm and encouragement. I am so lucky to call you a mentor, a role model, and a friend. To everyone

I worked with at Interfaith Youth Core—you all deserve individual shout-outs because each of you has done so much for me, but please know that you are all over this book. It is no exaggeration to say that *Faitheist* exists entirely because of each of you.

Greg Epstein—Thanks for inspiring me to gamble on this work and move halfway across the country to pursue it in Humanist community, even though we had no guarantees it would pan out. You took a chance on me, and I won't soon forget that. Sarah Chandonnet—You are an unsung hero, and I'm grateful to call you my colleague and friend. John Figdor—We've butted heads and found surprising common ground, and I think we're both better for it. James Croft—You're brash and brilliant; you keep me on my toes and challenge me to be more thoughtful, and I'm so indebted to you for it. To all of the HCH students and general community— you all motivate me and teach me so much. I love our scrappy, earnest, caring, action-oriented community.

Joshua Stanton, Stephanie Varnon-Hughes, Ian Burzynski, Honna Eichler, Alisa Roadcup, Or Rose, Jenny Peace, and everyone at the *Journal of Inter-Religious Dialogue*—I'm proud of the work we've done together to help create spaces where people can be in conversation with one another. Thank you for helping me find my own footing alongside you, and for carrying that vision forward.

To the people who helped me wrangle this into an actual book with their compassionate and frank edits: Amy Caldwell—Thanks for going to bat for this project and helping me turn it into a book. You're incredible at what you do and working with you has been a thrill. Let's do it again someday. Serah Blain—You inspire me with the thoughtfulness of your words and your actions, and I'd be lost without you. Karla McLaren—You live and breathe empathy, and without yours this project wouldn't have happened. Nat DeLuca—You are wise beyond our cumulative years, and your feedback kept me laughing and optimistic. Chelsea Link—Your future is limitless; thank you for the edits, for our work together, and for your friendship. Sam Lansky—Thanks for pushing me to dream bigger at the moment I needed to be pushed most, dear friend. Everyone at Beacon—Your confidence in and commitment to this project was, in my eyes, unmerited . . . thank you for it. I couldn't be happier to be a member of the Beacon family.

To my many friends and colleagues in the atheist, skeptic, and Humanist movements, the interfaith movement, and the LGBT community—Thank you for your bold dedication to truth and compassion, for standing up for cooperation in a world that tells us that we are supposed to be enemies, and for keeping me sane every day. I could write thousands of words thanking you all by name, but I have limited space and there just aren't enough words to communicate how much you all inspire me with your courage and vision.

Kate Sutlief, Matthew Martin, Ross Murray, my TEC friends, and all of the people I met as a Christian who continue to love and support me without hesitation—thank you for continuing to live out the values that initially brought me into the community.

To my professors, advisors, and classmates at Meadville Lombard, Augsburg, and the various seminaries I took courses at—You taught me more than any book could communicate. To my peers and professors at Loyola's Institute of Pastoral Studies—Much of my work and this book is a direct outgrowth of what I uncovered while studying alongside you.

To those who've helped me grow up and out at pivotal moments: Erik Roldan—I will always treasure the time I spent with you in Chicago. You were my rock, and I miss you all the time. Ky Dickens—You're fiery, brilliant, and so generous. You are the person I want to be when I grow up. Joey Blaha—Looking back on my Chicago years, I think of how you were always there for me. You're an amazing human being. Jena Roth—No friend has been there as consistently and sympathetically as you. We're in this for life. Kaitlin Barnes—Your love and laughter give me so much joy, and you were indescribably patient and kind during some of the worst times. Valarie Kaur—I've probably told you that you are one of the people I most admire more times than anyone should, but it's absolutely true. Joanna Ware—Thanks for being a constant resource, respite, ally, and inspiration. Alex Dakoulas—You came into my life at an inopportune time, but it turned out to be the perfect time. Thank you for reminding me just how magical the universe can be.

There are *so* many other people I need to thank—people who have contributed so much to my life—but I am short on words. Please don't let my brevity suggest that you weren't an integral part of the process. Walker Bristol, Stephen Goeman, Charlotte Arsenault, Vlad Chituc, Michael De Dora, Conrad Hudson, Lucy Gubbins, Nate Gottfried, Bryan and Natalie Parys, Oliver Goodrich, Tim Dougherty, Alex Small, Malena Thoson, Davey Ball, Nate Beske, Kari Aanestad, Beau Sorenson, Bruce Johansen, Grant Hanna, Ben Lundquist, Mark Mann, Corinne Tobias, Dan Polyak, Emily Hauser, Kate Fridkis Berring, Justin Kutzer, Robert Chlala, Emily Papke-Larson, Nick Mattos, Ali McDonald, Amy Nicole Miller, Shaylah Fawn DeViney, Jake Thompson, Dale McGowan, Daniel Loxton, Josh Rosenau, John Shook, Sarah Hippolitus, Andrew Lovley, Nathan Dunbar, Heidi Anderson, Jeff Wagg, Leo Lincourt, Barbara Drescher, Kevin Watson, Hemant Mehta, Ed Beck, Eric

Haaland, Anne Klaeysen, Tim Pate, Kayley Whalen, Jason Loxton, Paula Allen, Marc Barnhill, Joey Haban, Nathan Bupp, Jason Tippitt, Jennifer Newport, Michael McRae, Michael Amini, Wendi Wheeler, Greg Kirby, Roy Natian, Amye Broyles, D. J. Grothe, Travis Prinslow, Rose St. Clair, Ed Clint, Dren Asselmeier, A. J. Kumar, Peter McLellan, Aaron Wells, Ted Fabel, Sean Stanhill, Jay Matchett, Brian Krohn, Rachel Storm, Alykhan Alani, Greg Dubow, Will Schultze, John Tolley, Leon Andrew Hensley, Mike Hogue, Susi Pangerl, Andrew Fogle, Simon Taylor, Kylie Sturgess, Jack Scanlan, Jason Ball, Meredith Doig, Leslie Cannold, Jayson Daniel Cooke, Matt Morris, Nick Cloutier, Katie Heaney, Brian Noy, Christopher Luna, Jon Richardson, Derek Webb, Chris Geidner, Joke Olateju, Jason Romero, Bradley Stern, Alex Goldschmidt, Chris LaTondresse, Andrew Marin, Lori Bradnt Hale, Cory Froehlich, Lia Bengston, Jake Schlichting, Matt Reyna, Chris Jacobs, Adam Garner, Frank Fredericks, Tim Brauhn, Joshua Eaton, Rachel Nelson, Greg Damhorst, Anthony Fatta, Kelsey Sheridan, Lauren Seganos, Mustafa Abdullah, Miranda Hovemeyer, Brian Halaas, Jahnabi Barooah, Simon Curtis, John Benutty, Mike Andreozzi, the 69½ JP crew, and so many others. Many of you have put up with worst in me and seen the best in me. I love you.

To the many musicians who soundtracked my writing—Without your music, I wouldn't have typed a single word. To those who have been extremely critical of my work—Thank you for giving me ample opportunities to reflect, refine, and reconsider. I'm deeply grateful. To those whose names are missing but belong here— Please forgive me. You know how scattered I can be. I'll get you on the next go-'round, my friends.

Notes

Foreword

1. PZ Myers, "Get Meaner, Angrier, Louder, Fiercer," Pharyngula, March 1, 2007, http://scienceblogs.com/pharyngula/.

1. There's Nothing Worse Than a Faitheist

1. Carl Sagan, *The Demon-Haunted World: Science as a Candle in the Dark* (New York: Random House, 1997), 300.
2. John L. Esposito and Dalia Mogahed, *Who Speaks for Islam? What a Billion Muslims Really Think* (New York: Gallup, 2008).
3. PZ Myers, "Molly Norris in Hiding," Pharyngula, September 16, 2010, http://scienceblogs.com/pharyngula/.
4. Marshall Ganz, "Why Stories Matter," *Sojourners*, March 2009, www.sojo.net/, accessed June 22, 2011.
5. Benedict Carey, "This Is Your Life (and How You Tell It)," *New York Times*, May 22, 2007, http://www.nytimes.com/, accessed June 19, 2010.
6. Eboo Patel, "Religion Today: Bomb, Barrier or Bridge?" *Huffington Post*, August 5, 2010, http://www.huffingtonpost.com/, accessed September 3, 2010.
7. Sam Harris, "Christian Terrorism and Islamophobia," July 24, 2011, *Sam Harris*, http://www.samharris.org/.
8. "The Millennials: Confident. Connected. Open to Change," Pew Research Center, February 24, 2010, http://pewresearch.org/, February 25, 2010.
9. Peter Berger, "What Happens When a Leftist Philosopher Discovers God?" *American Interest*, September 21, 2011, http://blogs.the-american-interest.com/, accessed October 14, 2011.
10. David M. Wulff, *Psychology of Religion: Classic and Contemporary*, 2nd ed. (New York: John Wiley & Sons, 1997), p. v.

2. Starting Secular, Seeking Substance

1. From *Present Moment Wonderful Moment*. Quoted in *A Lifetime of Peace: Essential Writings by and about Thich Nhat Hanh*, Jennifer Schwamm Willis, ed. (Cambridge, MA: Da Capo Press, 2003), 141.

2. Jan N. Gretlund and Karl-Heinz Westarp, *Flannery O'Connor's Radical Reality* (Columbia: University of South Carolina, 2006), p. 39.

3. Conversion and Confusion

1. Tim LaHaye and Jerry B. Jenkins, *Nicolae: The Rise of the Antichrist* (Carol Stream, IL: Tyndale House, 1998), p. 240.
2. Larry Richards and Sue Poorman Richards, *The Teen Study Bible: New International Version* (Grand Rapids, MI: Zondervan, 1998), p. 1515.
3. Ibid., p. 140.

6. Putting My Money Where Other People's Mouths Are

1. Eboo Patel, *Acts of Faith: The Story of an American Muslim, the Struggle for the Soul of a Generation* (Boston: Beacon, 2007), p. 181.
2. William R. White, *Speaking in Stories: Resources for Christian Storytellers* (Minneapolis: Augsburg, 1982), p. 8.

7. In Search of the Secular Soul

1. "Humanist Manifesto III," American Humanist Association, 2003, http://www.americanhumanist.org/, accessed November 30, 2011.
2. Kurt Vonnegut, *Palm Sunday: An Autobiographical Collage* (New York: Dial, 2011), p. 180.
3. Hemant Mehta, "What Can Atheists Learn from the LGBT Movement?" *Friendly Atheist* blog, Patheos.com, August 6, 2010.
4. Barry A. Kosmin and Ariela Keysar, "American Religious Identification Survey (ARIS 2008) Summary Report," March 2009, http://commons.trincoll.edu/, accessed July 7, 2011.
5. James Joyner, "Black President More Likely than Mormon or Atheist," *Outside the Beltway*, February 20, 2007, http://www.outsidethebeltway.com/, accessed August 30, 2010.
6. Laura Sheahen, "Why Religion Must End: Interview with Sam Harris," *Beliefnet*, August 18, 2011, http://www.beliefnet.com/.
7. Chris Hedges, *I Don't Believe in Atheists* (New York: Free Press, 2008), pp. 1–2.
8. Reza Aslan, "Harris, Hitchens, Dawkins, Dennett: Evangelical Atheists?" *On Faith* blog, *Washington Post* online, July 16, 2010, http://newsweek.washingtonpost.com/, accessed October 17, 2010.
9. PZ Myers, "Perspective," *Internet Archive: Pharyngula*, March 1, 2007, http://scienceblogs.com/pharyngula/, accessed November 20, 2011.
10. "*Chris Stedman, PZ Myers, Leslie Cannold: Can Believers & Atheists Work Together for the Common Good?*" transcript, 2012 Global Atheist Convention Official Fringe Event, "The Road Less Traveled: Can Believers and Atheists Work Together for the Common Good?" http://soundcloud.com/.

11. "Free Church Ministers in Anglican Pulpits. Dr Temple's Call: The South India Scheme," *Guardian*, May 26, 1943.

12. Lauri Lebo, "New Theory for Tucson Tragedy: Blame the Atheists," *Religion Dispatches*, January 11, 2011, http://www.religiondispatches.org/, accessed January 11, 2011.

13. Jamison Foser, "CNN's Erickson Suggests Government Should Not 'Accommodate' Atheists," *Media Matters for America*, January 11, 2011, http://mediamatters.org/.

14. "What Are The Goals of the Atheist Movement?" *Greta Christina's Blog*, December 21, 2011, http://freethoughtblogs.com/greta.

15. Greta Christina, "What Can the Atheist Movement Learn from the Gay Movement?" *Greta Christina's Blog*, February 15, 2010, http://gretachristina.typepad.com/.

16. Tom Rees, "Atheists Are Disagreeable and Unconscientious," *Epiphenom: The Science of Religion and Non-Belief*, March 4, 2010, http://epiphenom.fieldofscience.com/, accessed September 3, 2011.

17. Ian Sample, "Stephen Hawking: 'There Is No Heaven; It's a Fairy Story,'" *Guardian*, May 15, 2011, http://www.guardian.co.uk/, accessed May 16, 2011.

8. Fact or Friction, Engage or Enrage

1. Martin Luther King Jr., *Where Do We Go from Here: Chaos or Community?* (Boston: Beacon Press, 1968), p. 67.

2. Alasdair C. MacIntyre, *After Virtue: A Study in Moral Theory* (Notre Dame, IN: University of Notre Dame, 2007), p. 216.

3. Eboo Patel and Cassie Meyer, "Defining Religious Pluralism: A Response to Robert McKim," *Journal of College and Character* 11, no. 2 (2010), http://journals.naspa.org/.

4. Interfaith Youth Core, *The Interfaith Leader's Toolkit* (Chicago: IFYC, 2009), p. 16.

5. Patel, *Acts of Faith*, p. xv.

6. Carl Sagan, *Cosmos* (New York: Random House, 1980), p. 339.

7. Lymari Morales, "Knowing Someone Gay/Lesbian Affects Views of Gay Issues," Gallup, May 29, 2009, http://www.gallup.com/, accessed August 8, 2010.

8. Bobby Ghosh, "Mosque Controversy: Does America Have a Muslim Problem?" *Time*, August 30, 2010, http://www.time.com/.

9. "Public Remains Conflicted Over Islam," Pew Research Center for the People and the Press, August 24, 2010, http://people-press.org.

10. "Speeches and Letters of Abraham Lincoln, 1832–1865," Amazon.com: Kindle Store, http://www.amazon.com/, accessed March 30, 2011.